COOKING
- IN A -
CASSEROLE

COOKING
- IN A -
CASSEROLE

Yvette Stachowiak and Katharine Blakemore

NOTE

1. All recipes serve four unless otherwise stated.

2. All spoon measurements are level. Spoon measures can be bought in both imperial and metric sizes to give accurate measurements of small quantities.

3. All eggs are sizes 2 or 3 unless otherwise stated.

4. All sugar is granulated unless otherwise stated.

5. Preparation times given are an average calculated during recipe testing.

6. Metric and imperial measurements have been calculated separately. Use one set of measurements only as they are not exact equivalents.

7. Cooking times may vary slightly depending on the individual oven and on the type of casserole dish used. Dishes should be placed in the centre of an oven unless otherwise specified.

8. Always preheat the oven or grill to the specified temperature.

9. If glass or cast iron enamelled casserole dishes, which conduct heat rapidly, are used, a 12°C (25°F) reduction in the cooking temperatures stated in the recipes should be made.

10. [F] indicates at which point a dish can be frozen. [A] indicates up to which point the dish can be prepared in advance. Brief freezing and/or advance preparation details can be found at the end of all recipes in which these symbols have been included.

11. If using a fan-assisted oven, follow the manufacturer's instructions for guidance on temperature adjustments.

First published in 1987 by Octopus Books Limited
Grosvenor Street, London, England

© 1987 Hennerwood Publications Limited
ISBN 0 86273 374 X

Printed in Great Britain

CONTENTS

INTRODUCTION

*A well-prepared casserole, that splendid
mainstay of our cuisine, can provide a
memorably flavoursome meal at minimal
expense or it can be the elegant centrepiece
around which a formal dinner party can be set. In
this introductory chapter to Cooking In a
Casserole the essence of the perfect casserole is
explored. There is a little bit of history, more
about the ideal shape of casserole dishes and about
the other utensils the cook may need and plenty
about the essential ingredients and additional
flavourings which can go into a casserole. There
is also a detailed analysis of how the basic
casserole is prepared, with hints on how it can be
varied to provide a seemingly limitless collection
of ideas for cooking in a casserole.*

A casserole can evoke many different memories. For some of us, it is a wonderful, warming one-dish meal on a cold winter evening. For others, it is traditional 'peasant' fare: inexpensive ingredients combined with care to provide a satisfying repast. Some think of a casserole as an easy way to enjoy the company of family and guests – it can simmer gently, and be virtually ignored while you join the family.

Culinary experts have long argued as to the exact definition of a casserole. Some believe the term refers to the cooking method, while others maintain that the cooking vessel defines a casserole. Still others think a casserole is both the cooking method and the vessel. The definition remains a broad one.

This collection of recipes encompasses two main types of casserole. In the first, a lidded container is used and the raw ingredients are slow-cooked. One of the benefits of cooking with a covered casserole is that it creates a self-basting action – the casserole produces steam which rises to the lid, then falls back on the meat. All the juices are well secured in the casserole and will be concentrated in the final sauce. Classic examples of this kind of casserole included in this book are Oxtail Casserole (page 73), Osso Bucco (page 76) and the French Daube (page 69).

In the second type, the basic casserole ingredients, sometimes pre-cooked, are frequently combined with starchy items such as potatoes, rice and pasta and the casserole can be cooked uncovered for part or all of the cooking time – an important difference. To protect the casserole ingredients from drying out, various toppings such as breadcrumbs or slices of bread and scones may be added during the cooking period. Examples of this kind of casserole in this book are Beef Cobbler (page 66), Carbonnade de Boeuf (page 67), Turkey Rice Casserole (page 60) and Smoked Haddock and Potato Casserole (page 53).

Both these types of casserole capitalize on the idea of easy cooking for the home chef. And today, when time and money are at such a premium, casseroles are a terrific way of maximising both.

There are two ways of cooking meat – either by 'dry' heat or by 'moist' heat. Dry heat methods include roasting, grilling, baking, frying and, in fact, deep-frying. Cuts like lamb chops, sirloin steak and veal scallopine, which are naturally tender, will not become any softer with cooking. These cuts, and many more, come from those parts of an animal which have the least amount of exercise and therefore only need the quick cooking of dry heat methods to present them at their best.

Boiling, poaching, steaming, pressure cooking and 'wrap' cooking (using foil, leaves or greaseproof paper) are examples of the moist heat method, as is casserole cooking.

Inexpensive cuts of meat, such as an oxtail or a sinewy neck piece, are prime candidates for the moist heat method of cooking. These cuts are tough because they come from the most exercised and, therefore, the most muscular parts of the animal, and thus will be best tenderized by a long, slow cooking process, such as is used in many casserole recipes.

Obviously, there are exceptions to this basic distinction, with some cuts, such as chops, leg steaks or chicken joints, being suited to cooking by both types of method.

THE HISTORY OF CASSEROLES

The historical development of casseroles is related to the availability of three essential items – fuel, cooking utensils and meat.

Adequate fuel, be it wood, coal, gas or electricity, is essential. Most of us do not have to worry about the availability of fuel, though its cost can be an important consideration: using a casserole is a potentially efficient use of fuel since it generally calls for a lowish temperature while the use of a closed dish allows other foods to be cooked in the oven at the same time.

Our ancestors cooked their meats by grilling over a fire so there was no need for an array of cooking vessels. The meats were either skewered and grilled or just placed in the embers. However, with the increasing availability of cooking utensils, made initially of bronze and pottery, cookery made rapid progress.

By the eighteenth century, casserole dishes were commonly used in France. However, the dishes were not used in the way they are today. For example, one eighteenth-century recipe was for scrambled eggs with cheese. You had 'to break and beat up the eggs in a casserole . . . (then) set the casserole over a brisk fire'. You could, even today, make scrambled eggs in this manner, but it used to be the dish, rather than the ingredients that defined the casserole.

Once you have a fire and a cooking pot, you still need the main ingredients that go into the casserole. The contemporary widespread availability of meat is an anomaly compared to even a century ago. With recent transportation and refrigeration developments, we are now able to purchase a wide array of first-class meats. What a change from the past when you were restricted to buying what was in season and what came to your market, with no guarantee as to its freshness nor of the conditions in which it had been kept.

Even when meat had become readily available, culinary knowledge did not extend to recognizing that different cuts of meat could benefit from different kinds of cooking treat-

ment. Grilling, roasting or boiling were the preferred treatments for all meats. Changing culinary fashions are traceable through old menus, however.

In 1571, the menu for a banquet celebrating the wedding of Master Baulde Cuvillon in France, had 35 savoury items on its menu. Out of these, only two were vaguely reminiscent of what we understand a casserole to be. By the eighteenth century, in a menu presented by Marshal the Duc de Richelieu, four out of the six entrées were cooked as casseroles.

So with the development of efficient fuels, cooking vessels and materials, combined with an increasing measure of experience, the casserole came to be.

CHOOSING A CASSEROLE DISH

When choosing a casserole, you will need to balance several important considerations, including size, shape, weight and the material the casserole is made from, so that you acquire the casserole most appropriate to your needs.

With the huge variety of casserole dishes now available, it is often not appropriate to state exactly which size should be used for any particular recipe. The following figures should help you, however:

600 ml–1.2 litres (1–2 pints) casserole dish serves 1–2 people;

1.2 litres–1.75 litres (2–3 pints) casserole dish serves 2–4 people;

1.75 litres–2.75 litres (3–5 pints) casserole dish serves 4–6 people.

A large casserole, holding 1.75–2.75 litres (3–5 pints) is ideal for cooking a family meal

If you are unsure of the measurement of your dish, fill it with water from a litre or pint measuring jug. You will now be able to gauge exactly how large it is.

Do bear in mind that the contents of a casserole will bubble over if it is too small. If, on the other hand, it is too large, the food can dry out. Also, deep casseroles need more cooking time than shallow casseroles because the greater surface area in the shallow container allows the heat to penetrate the casserole that much faster.

The shape of a casserole dish is important. Food will cook more evenly in round and oval dishes than in square or rectangular ones, in which the corners may burn. In addition, glass or dark enamel dishes tend to hold the heat more than metal ones.

A casserole needs a tight-fitting lid if it is to benefit from the self-basting method. The lid should also be easy to grasp with an oven mitt or some form of hand protection. If a casserole has lost its lid, it can be tightly covered with foil, which makes an adequate substitute. Just be careful when you remove the foil, since steam, which burns badly as its temperature is much higher than boiling water, will probably have built up underneath. Carefully remove the foil with oven mitts, lifting the corner furthest away from you and standing well back to protect your face.

A casserole must also have good handles to allow safe, easy transfer from the stove top or oven to the table. Again, make sure you can grip the handles while you are wearing oven mitts. Obviously, it is important that the

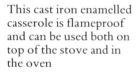

This cast iron enamelled casserole is flameproof and can be used both on top of the stove and in the oven

casserole's handles are both ovenproof and flameproof – no wood or plastic.

Whatever the shape of a casserole dish, its weight is of prime importance. The heavier the casserole, the thicker the sides and bottom of the dish will be. As you are aiming for slow, even cooking, you should try to get a dish which conducts heat efficiently and *slowly*. Therefore, buy the heaviest casserole dishes you can afford and easily handle.

Casserole dishes may be made out of various materials, including earthenware, cast iron with an enamelled finish, plain cast iron, glass, aluminium and other light metals, and copper.

Some casserole dishes are only ovenproof, while others are flameproof as well. So what's the difference? Ovenproof means you can put the dish in the oven without fear of its breaking during cooking. Earthenware, china, glass and pottery casseroles are ovenproof. Flameproof casseroles, such as enamelled and cast iron ones, can be used to cook ingredients on top of the stove as well as in the oven. They can be used to sear or brown-off the ingredients of a casserole before putting the dish in the oven to cook; with an ovenproof casserole, this process would have to be done in a separate pan and the ingredients transferred to the casserole.

With a glass or cast iron enamelled casserole dish, it must be remembered that both types need a 12°C (25°F) reduction in the cooking temperatures stated in this book because of their rapid conductivity and heat-retaining qualities. As well as reducing the cooking temperature, it is important to keep a close eye on the casserole while it is cooking to prevent burning.

SOME CLASSIC CASSEROLE DISHES

Perhaps the most famous classic casserole dish is the daubière. Cooking 'en daube' is a traditional French braising method. Today's daubières are glazed earthenware with a deep, bulbous shape, though in the past they were also made from stoneware or copper. The neck is smaller than the rest of the pot so that evaporation is kept to a minimum and the fat collects on the top for easy removal.

Another classic pot is the marmite. This is basically a large, straight-sided pot, almost as high as it is wide, with handles and a lid. The materials used to construct a marmite include glazed earthenware, stainless steel, copper and aluminium. If you are using an earthenware marmite, it should not be used on the top of the stove unless it is protected from direct heat by a heat-diffusing pad. (A 'petite marmite' is not a smaller version of the pot, but the name given to a beef-based savoury soup served in a small earthenware pot.)

A bean pot, another often-used classic casser-ole pot, is usually made from glazed earthen-ware, has a tight-fitting lid and, like the marmite, is about as tall as it is broad.

The traditional Moroccan stew, or tagine, is cooked in a dish called a tagine. This is a round, shallow, earthenware pot with a tall, conical lid. It may sometimes be found in kitchenware shops in this country.

CARING FOR YOUR CASSEROLE

Casseroles which are only ovenproof need particular care; quick and drastic temperature changes can shatter the dish. Do not take a cold dish and put it into a preheated oven or under hot running water, as it may break. By the same token, do not place a hot ovenproof dish straight into the refrigerator or freezer. The fridge or freezer temperature will rise (possibly affecting other food), the dish will shatter and the casserole will be a complicated mess to clear up.

Cleaning any kind of casserole dish is re-latively easy. Only if food sticks to the dish or burns will you have problems. If your dish is stained, it is best to fill it with warm water, add a little washing-up liquid and let it sit over-night. It should come out sparkling clean with the aid of a nylon scourer.

Do not scour cast iron casserole dishes – just use the warm water and detergent soaking tip. Never use any abrasives on a non-stick surface. With a little care in the beginning, your dish should be as clean as the day you bought it.

Unglazed earthenware casseroles and lids should be soaked in water for 15 minutes before you add your ingredients. When your dish is in the oven, the clay releases a steam which keeps the ingredients from drying out and bastes them. As unglazed clay is porous, fish should not be cooked in it or the smell will permanent-ly impregnate the casserole.

When you take your casserole to the table, it's a good idea to place it on one of the many kinds of protective mat available to guard against damaging the surface of the table.

TOOLS FOR CASSEROLES

Once you have the appropriate casserole dishes, what else do you need? First, you might consider buying tongs for removing the meat and turning it while browning. This is better than using a fork, which could pierce the meat and cause it to lose essential juices. Whisks, wooden spoons, slotted spoons and stainless steel colanders are also helpful, but the beauty of casserole cookery is that the necessary implements are kept to a minimum.

THE STANDARD CASSEROLE

There is a basic formula for casserole cookery. With few exceptions, once you've learned how to make one, you could make them all. The standard method for the assembly and cooking of a casserole follows.

As inexpensive cuts of meat are frequently the main ingredients of a casserole, it is a good idea to marinate the meat for several hours before making the casserole to give it extra tenderness and flavour. Acidic elements, such as vinegar, wine and lemon juice, are added to the marinade to help break down the tough meat fibres. Flavourings for the marinade include carrots, onions, garlic, herbs and spices.

Whether the meat has been marinated or not, it tends to be moist before you start cooking. As the next step involves searing the meat over a high temperature to lock in all the juices, the meat benefits from being dried first with paper towels. Otherwise, you might find that the meat 'stews' rather than browns.

To sear or brown the meat, a little oil or a combination of oil and butter are heated in a flameproof casserole or pan. The meat is then added and turned frequently over a high heat until browned on all sides. This guarantees tenderness and full-flavoured meat.

The meat is then usually removed from the casserole or pan and set aside. Sliced vegetables, such as onions, leeks, carrots and garlic are added to the casserole dish. These are then cooked, or 'sweated', for a few minutes. Their juices will be amalgamated into the final sauce for the casserole.

The meat is returned to the casserole and a liquid and seasonings are added. The liquid could be a stock, wine, liqueur or a sauce, such as a white sauce, brown sauce or tomato sauce. Then comes the easy part – you cover the casserole and let it go about its business for the next hour or so, checking it occasionally to make sure all is well.

When the casserole has finished cooking, there may be a layer of fat on the top, particularly if the meat in the casserole is lamb or duck, both of which are fatty meats. To remove the fat, or 'degrease' the casserole, you have several options. You can tilt the casserole slightly by placing one corner on an upturned saucer. After a few minutes, the fat will have gathered in the tilted corner and should be easily removed with a spoon.

If there is only a thin layer of fat, paper towels may get it off. Just place a sheet of the paper flat on top of the casserole and let the fat be absorbed. Repeat this until all the fat has been removed. Finally, a bulb baster can also be used to suck the fat up from the surface. If you are using a plastic one, make sure the liquid is not boiling hot.

Once you've removed the fat from your liquid, you will have to check whether it needs thickening or not. Some casseroles have plain flour sprinkled on to the meat when it is returned to the dish after searing. These casseroles usually do not need any more attention. If, however, you feel the sauce is still too thin, you can always reduce it over a high heat until it has the desired consistency, though the other ingredients of the casserole must be removed first and kept warm.

If there has been no starch introduced to the casserole in the initial cooking process, it may need thickening. The normal procedure is to remove the meat and vegetables from the casserole to keep warm. You can then reduce the liquid or add a starch. You have several options. Flour, cornflour or arrowroot can be combined with a little liquid, such as stock or wine, until smooth. This paste is then stirred into the boiling cooking liquid and cooked for a few minutes. You should now have a smooth and thickened sauce.

Another method of using flour to thicken the cooking liquid involves kneading equal amounts of flour and butter together to form a 'beurre manié'. Small pieces of the beurre manié are stirred into the cooking liquid and allowed to cook, thickening the sauce.

Dairy products may also be used to thicken a sauce. Double cream is popular, and, nowadays, soured cream or Greek-style plain yogurt. Care must be taken with the latter as it breaks down if allowed to boil. Yogurt can be 'stabilized', so that it does not break down, by adding a teaspoon of cornflour per 300 ml (½ pint) of yogurt. Double cream may also be combined with egg yolks to form a 'liaison' which will thicken the casserole. Again, low heat is imperative when mixing in the liaison, or you will end up with scrambled eggs.

This is the stage at which the dish should be checked for taste and the seasoning adjusted, if necessary.

The sauce is now finished and the meat and vegetables have been returned to the casserole. There is only one thing left – the garnish. Remembering that people eat with their eyes first, a garnish is essential. It does not have to be anything fancy as even a sprinkling of chopped parsley will enliven the plainest-looking casserole. See page 14 for ideas for quick and easy garnishes. Now, for the moment though, you can sit down and enjoy your creation.

CUTS OF MEAT FOR CASSEROLES

With a few exceptions, tougher (and inexpensive) cuts of meat and poultry are most suitable for casserole cooking. The following is a list of some common cuts you should be looking for:
1) Beef – braising steak, chuck (shoulder) steak, flank steak, mince, oxtail and offals;
2) Lamb – middle neck, breast, braising lamb and offal;

3) Veal – pie (casserole) veal;
4) Pork – pork shoulder steaks, braising pork, prime collar bacon joint, offal and sausages;
5) Chicken – boiling hens, whole and jointed chicken and offal;
6) Turkey – jointed turkey pieces.

There are other kinds of animal produce which are also suitable for cooking in a casserole, though they may be more expensive. These include:

1) Veal – shin of veal and offal;
2) Bacon joints;
3) Duck and goose – whole or jointed roasting ducks and geese;
4) Game – venison, rabbit, hare, pheasant, grouse and pigeons;
5) Fish – all types of shellfish, saltwater and freshwater fish, though not usually in long, slowly cooked casseroles.

Names of various cuts can vary from region to region. If you are in doubt at the butcher's shop or fishmonger's, describe exactly what you want to do with your purchase. He or she should be able to guide you.

VEGETABLE COOKERY IN CASSEROLES

Vegetables, being nutritious, economical and healthy foods, are playing an increasingly large part in our cooking and many delicious vegetable dishes can be cooked in a casserole.

While root vegetables such as carrots, potatoes, parsnips, turnips and Jerusalem artichokes are ideal candidates for the longer, slower cooking techniques of casserole cookery, many other, more exotic vegetables such as fennel, chicory, okra, pumpkin and squashes also benefit from being cooked in a casserole. They retain their shape and absorb accompanying flavours well, so that, with clever use of herbs

Illustrating the great variety of casserole cooking: a whole chicken cooked with vegetables and meat with a dumpling topping

and spices, vegetable casseroles need never be bland or uninteresting.

Beans and other pulses, too, once they have had an initial rapid boiling for at least 10 minutes on top of the stove, benefit similarly from being cooked in a casserole in the oven.

Casseroles can be used to cook both main course vegetarian meals and vegetable accompaniments, such as carrots, cabbage and broccoli, in the oven when it is on for another purpose, thus increasing their value as economic foods.

SEASONING CASSEROLES

Both fresh and dried herbs can be used to season a casserole. Fresh herbs are preferred, but not always available. Dried herbs are acceptable as long as they have not been stored for more than 3 months. Use only half of the amount indicated for fresh herbs. Common herbs used in casserole cookery include parsley, chives, bay leaves, rosemary, dill, marjoram, sage, savory, thyme, oregano, basil, tarragon, coriander and chervil.

Spices are also important for flavouring a casserole. We all know pepper, but we should not forget mustard seeds, nutmeg, cloves, caraway seeds, chilli peppers, cumin, paprika, cayenne pepper, fennel seeds, dill seeds, cinnamon, ginger, turmeric, saffron, coriander, allspice, fenugreek, juniper berries and star anise.

As for salt, try to buy sea-salt as it is not so refined as ordinary salt. Wholefood pundits say it is better for us and it also tastes better.

A bouquet garni is frequently used while cooking a casserole. It can be purchased in a ready-made form, but with little effort and expense, you can make your own. The most common bouquet garni includes parsley stems, thyme, black peppercorns and a bay leaf wrapped in cheesecloth or muslin, then tied. It is placed in the casserole at the beginning of the cooking process and discarded after cooking.

GARNISHING CASSEROLES

Other than the ubiquitous parsley and watercress garnishes – and there's nothing wrong with them – you can add many other items to garnish a casserole. Pitted green and black olives and stuffed olives can be used, either whole or sliced. Lemon garnishes are popular for fish and veal dishes. Slices, twists, crowns and rind of lemon can decorate a casserole.

Some of the herbs and spices which can flavour casseroles: 1 Rosemary, 2 Thyme, 3 Tarragon, 4 Sorrel, 5 Mint, 6 Marjoram, 7 Oregano, 8 Sage, 9 Lemon Grass, 10 Juniper Berries, 11 Parsley, 12 Garlic, 13 Fennel, 14 Ginger, 15 Coriander, 16 Dill, 17 Chives, 18 Chervil, 19 Bay, 20 Carraway

Avocado slices or fans, brushed with lemon juice to prevent discolouring, or cucumber twists are nice touches for fish casseroles and artfully arranged sprigs of chives and/or thin slivers of red peppers can be a fabulous garnish. Apple or other fruit slices are particularly well-suited to pork and ham dishes. Toasted nuts and seeds or croûtons can provide a satisfying crunch for those casseroles which consist of 'soft' ingredients such as some fish, or vegetables which have been cooked for a long time. And swirls of cream or Greek-style plain yogurt can top your casserole.

As long as you keep in mind the flavours of your casserole, a complimentary garnish is limited only by your imagination.

COOLING AND CHILLING CASSEROLES

Some casseroles benefit from an overnight chilling period. While the flavours become more intense, the fat can also be easily discarded as it hardens into a simple-to-remove layer.

There are a few rules to keep in mind when cooling and chilling a casserole. Never place a casserole directly from the oven or stove top into your fridge or freezer because it could cause the temperature to rise dangerously, affecting the food already inside. A casserole should be allowed to cool completely before it is covered and stored. You can quickly finish off cooling a casserole (the faster, the better to prevent the growth of bacteria) by placing it into a sink partially filled with iced water. Just make sure you don't sink your casserole and that the casserole is not hot from the oven, if it is an ovenproof casserole. (For notes on reheating cooled and chilled casseroles see page 16.)

FREEZING CASSEROLES

Casseroles lend themselves very well to freezing and can be valuable items in your freezer. While cooking one particular casserole, why not use the oven space to cook another one and freeze it. You'll have a ready meal for those days when the last thing you want to do is cook. Another benefit of freezing casseroles is that it allows you to take advantage of seasonal

Most casseroles freeze well; here two batches from a larger casserole are being prepared for the freezer

foods and savour them year round.

There are several important rules for freezing casseroles. Do not freeze those containing frozen and thawed meat, raw rice and raw vegetables. (Frozen meat which has been thawed for using in a casserole and then cooked, can be refrozen so long as the process has been carried out as quickly as possible.) In addition, you should not freeze any casserole which contains: a thickened sauce, hard-boiled eggs, avocados, mayonnaise, soured cream, cream, cucumbers and any starches such as pasta or rice and potatoes, except for mashed potatoes. Do not freeze a topping – such as breadcrumbs – on a casserole as it can go soggy. Before you think there isn't a casserole left you can freeze, remember you can add most of the above items after your casserole has thawed.

You should also be sparing with the seasonings, including garlic, in casseroles that are to be frozen. Freezing acts as a long marination period and flavours may become too intense. It's best to underseason before freezing, then add to taste after you have reheated it.

You obviously do not want to lose a casserole dish in the Arctic depths of your freezer for a few months at a time. It's a good idea to line an appropriate dish with clingfilm, then foil. When your casserole is assembled (cooked and chilled, if necessary), tip the contents into the prepared container, wrap over the foil and freeze. Allow 2.5 cm (1 inch) head space for expansion while freezing. Once the casserole is frozen, you can lift it out of the dish, remove the container and return the foil parcel to the freezer – already pre-wrapped. Don't forget to label it for both the content and date of freezing.

Now that the casserole is safely ensconced in the freezer, you may wonder for how long it can be frozen. Here is a rule of thumb – if your casserole contains bacon, ham, pork or offal, it can be frozen for 1-2 months; other casseroles can be safely frozen for 3-4 months.

THAWING AND REHEATING CASSEROLES

To thaw a casserole before cooking, place it overnight in the fridge. If you have forgotten to remove the dish from the freezer, it can be put directly, uncovered, in a 150°C, 300°F, Gas Mark 2 oven for 1½-2 hours, though the oven should not be preheated, to prevent too great a temperature change. Don't forget to remove any plastic wrappings first and to stir the casserole regularly while cooking to ensure even heating.

Whether cooking a thawed casserole or reheating one after chilling it overnight, the procedure is the same. After the casserole has been taken out of the refrigerator, it should be

Opposite: the microwave has proved invaluable for thawing and reheating frozen casseroles

allowed to stand at room temperature for 30 minutes so that it reaches the temperature of 20°C (70°F). Place in an oven preheated to 170°C, 325°F, Gas Mark 3 and cook until thoroughly hot. Stir frequently while reheating so the heat has a chance to penetrate evenly.

Some casseroles can also be reheated on top of the stove. Again, allow the food to come to room temperature. Reheat over a medium-low heat, stirring frequently to prevent sticking. Serve only when the casserole is piping hot.

One problem about reheating a casserole is that the liquid it was cooked in can be absorbed by the main ingredients. Therefore, a reheated casserole may have less sauce than if it had been served immediately. To prevent this, an additional 50 ml (2 fl oz) of an appropriate liquid may be stirred into the casserole at the beginning of the reheating process.

MICROWAVING FROZEN CASSEROLES

Microwave cookers are helpful for thawing and reheating frozen casseroles. Before you start microwaving, any plastic wrap or foil surrounding the casserole should be discarded.

For a standard 4-serving frozen casserole, it should be cooked at 100% power (high) for approximately 10 minutes, giving it a ¼ turn. Reduce the power to 50% (medium) and continue to cook for 10 minutes. Stir frequently. Return the power to 100% (high) and stir well. Cook for 5-10 minutes until heated through. Stir every 2 minutes during the last cooking period. These times are approximate as they can vary considerably depending on the type of microwave cooker and its wattage and on the ingredients in the casserole. Check frequently and make a note of the results for future reference.

If you intend to reheat your casserole in a microwave, make sure it is in a dish which does not contain any metal or gold leaf trim.

FINAL HINT FOR CASSEROLE COOKERY

While cooking a casserole in your oven, you could add jacket potatoes to bake, a vegetable dish or even a pudding. Not only will you use your oven to its maximum efficiency, but you will also have little last-minute cooking to concern yourself with. As long as you do not overcrowd your oven, you will be saving money on your fuel bills.

Now you should be well-versed in casserole cookery. Enjoy the following recipes and don't be afraid to add your own touches. Recipes are really just guidelines that should be followed, but not rigidly. For the first attempt, it is best to adhere to the recipe; the next time you may well prefer to add your own variations.

DEFROST			POWER LEVEL
CHICKEN PORTIONS	1 lb.	10 mins	3
PORK CHOPS (4)	1¼ lb.	10 mins	3
STEAK	8 ozs.	5 mins	3
SAUSAGES	1 lb.	7 mins	3
MINCE	1 lb.	8 mins	3
TROUT	1 lb.	9 mins	3
REHEAT			
COFFEE	8 fl.ozs.	1 min	9
SOUP	10 fl.ozs.	3 mins	8
CASSEROLE	2 pints.	12 mins	8
VEGETABLES	12 ozs.	3 mins	8
MEAT PIE	5 ozs.	1¼ mins	8
PLATED MEAL	9 ins.	3 mins	8
COOK			
CHICKEN PORTIONS	1 lb.	10 mins	7
ROOT VEGETABLES	1 lb.	10 mins	9
PEAS	8 ozs.	5 mins	9
TROUT	1 lb.	5 mins	9
BACON	4 ozs.	4 mins	9
CAKE MIX	11.6 ozs.	5 mins	9

COOK

ER-674

EVERYDAY DISHES

These tasty family recipes are based on a variety
of generally less expensive meats, poultry and
fish. Sometimes the basic meats are cooked
whole, as in the recipes for Chicken in a Tureen
or Gingered Pot Roast; sometimes the meat is
turned into meatballs, as in the deliciously spiced
Swedish Meatballs, or into stuffings for
vegetables like peppers or cabbage, or jointed and
cooked with pasta or dumplings to provide
nutritious and budget-conscious meals. Children
should enjoy dishes like the Baked Bean
Casserole or the Chicken and Sausage
Casserole, while even the most critical adult
should warm to the splendid aroma arising from a
casserole filled with Piquant Beef Shortribs,
Veal Ragoût or Somerset Chicken.

PIQUANT BEEF SHORT RIBS

2 tablespoons vegetable oil
1½ kg (3 lb) beef short ribs or pork spareribs, cut into serving pieces
1 medium onion, peeled and finely chopped
350 ml (12 fl oz) tomato ketchup
250 ml (8 fl oz) water
50 ml (2 fl oz) red wine vinegar
1 garlic clove, peeled and finely chopped
3 tablespoons Worcestershire sauce
2 tablespoons sugar
1 tablespoon Dijon mustard
salt

PREPARATION TIME: 15 minutes
COOKING TIME: 2¼ hours
OVEN: 180°C, 350°F, Gas Mark 4

1 Heat the oil in a large flameproof casserole over a medium high heat. Add the ribs and onion and brown for 10 minutes.

2 Combine the remaining ingredients in a medium size bowl. Pour over the ribs, stirring well to coat. Cover the casserole and cook in a preheated oven for 2 hours until tender. [A]

3 Remove the excess fat and serve the casserole immediately with jacket potatoes and coleslaw.

[A] This recipe can be prepared the day before: chilling overnight enables the fat to be removed easily. Reheat, covered, at 180°C, 350°F, Gas Mark 4 for 30 minutes.

CHICKEN IN A TUREEN

1 celery heart
1 × 1¾ kg (4 lb) roasting chicken, tied, wing tips removed
1.75 litres (3 pints) chicken stock
1.75 litres (3 pints) water
4 young carrots, peeled
4 small onions, peeled
4 small turnips, trimmed
4 small leeks, white part only and tied in a bundle
12 parsley sprigs
1 sprig fresh thyme
1 bay leaf
salt
freshly ground black pepper
50 g (2 oz) butter
50 g (2 oz) plain flour
2 tablespoons finely chopped fresh parsley, to garnish

PREPARATION TIME: 30 minutes
COOKING TIME: 1¾ hours

1 Stuff the celery heart inside the chicken. Place the chicken in a large flameproof casserole. Cover with the stock and water. Bring slowly to the boil removing the scum when necessary. Cover and simmer for 15 minutes.

2 Reduce the heat to medium-low. Add the carrots, onions, turnips and leeks to the casserole. Place the parsley, thyme and bay leaf in a piece of cheesecloth and tie securely to make a bouquet garni. Place the bouquet garni in the casserole; season with salt and pepper. Cover and simmer the casserole for 1 hour.

3 Transfer the chicken and the vegetables to a heated serving platter. Remove the string from the chicken and the leeks.

4 Strain the cooking liquid, discarding the bouquet garni. Place 900 ml (1½ pints) of the liquid in a medium saucepan, reserving the remainder for another use. Bring the liquid to the boil over a high heat. Combine the butter and flour to make a beurre manié. While stirring, drop small pieces of the beurre manié into the boiling liquid. Cook for 5 minutes, until the sauce is smooth and thick. Taste and adjust the seasoning, if necessary. Transfer the sauce to a sauceboat.

5 Garnish the chicken with parsley.

STEWED CHICKEN WITH SPRING VEGETABLES

SERVES 8
75 g (3 oz) butter
3 tablespoons vegetable oil
1 × 2 kg (4½ lb) boiling hen, cut into 8 pieces
1 medium carrot, peeled and finely chopped
1 large onion, peeled and finely chopped
1 celery stick, finely chopped
900 ml (1½ pints) chicken stock
250 ml (8 fl oz) dry white wine
12 small onions, peeled
6 small carrots, peeled and cut into short lengths
6 small turnips, peeled and cut into cubes
6 small new potatoes, halved
3 tablespoons finely chopped fresh chervil
2 tablespoons finely chopped fresh basil
1 tablespoon fresh thyme leaves
1 teaspoon finely chopped fresh tarragon
1 bay leaf
225 g (8 oz) broccoli florets
100 g (4 oz) thawed frozen peas or cooked fresh peas
salt
freshly ground black pepper
3 egg yolks
120 ml (4 fl oz) double cream

Clockwise from left:
Piquant Beef Short Ribs;
Chicken in a Tureen;
Stewed Chicken with
Spring Vegetables

PREPARATION TIME: 40 minutes
COOKING TIME: 2¾ hours

1 Heat 3 tablespoons of the butter and the oil in a large frying pan over a medium-high heat. Add the chicken pieces, skin side down, and brown for 10 minutes, turning occasionally. Remove the chicken from the pan with a slotted spoon or tongs and place in a large flameproof casserole.

2 Pour off all but 3 tablespoons of the fat from the frying pan. Add the carrot, onion and celery. Reduce the heat to medium, then cook for 10 minutes, stirring frequently. Add 250 ml (8 fl oz) of the stock, then bring to the boil. Boil, scraping the bottom to incorporate all the bits, for 3 minutes. Pour the mixture over the chicken in the casserole.

3 Add the remaining stock and wine to the casserole. Bring to the boil over a medium heat, then reduce the heat to a simmer. Cook the chicken, partially covered, for 1½ hours, removing the scum occasionally.

4 Melt the remaining butter in a large frying pan over a medium-high heat. Add the onions, carrots, turnips and potatoes. Cook, stirring frequently, for 10 minutes until lightly browned. Transfer the mixture with a slotted spoon to the casserole. Add the chervil, basil, thyme, tarragon and bay leaf. Cook for 15–25 minutes, until the chicken and vegetables are tender. [A] Add the broccoli and peas. Cook for 4–5 minutes until they are tender.

5 Remove the chicken and vegetables to a heated deep platter with a slotted spoon. Keep warm.

6 Skim the fat off the casserole. Remove the bay leaf. Add the salt and pepper to taste. Using a whisk, thoroughly combine the egg yolks and cream in a medium bowl. Whisk in 120 ml (4 fl oz) of the hot cooking liquid. Slowly stir the egg mixture into the casserole. Cook over a very low heat for 3 minutes, stirring constantly, until thickened. Do not boil.

7 Pour the sauce over the chicken. Serve immediately with warm French bread.

[A] Can be prepared up to a day in advance, covered and kept chilled. Reheat over a medium-low heat for 15–20 minutes until the chicken is hot before continuing with the recipe.

VEAL RAGOÛT

SERVES 6

2 tablespoons vegetable oil
1 kg (2 lb) stewing veal, cubed
3 tablespoons plain flour
1 garlic clove, peeled and finely chopped
900 ml (1½ pints) chicken stock
2 tablespoons tomato purée
1 tablespoon finely chopped fresh parsley
1 tablespoon fresh thyme leaves or ½ teaspoon dried thyme
1 bay leaf, crushed
salt
freshly ground black pepper
40 g (1½ oz) butter
3 medium onions, peeled and quartered
4 medium carrots, peeled and cut into 2½ cm (1 inch) pieces
1 tablespoon sugar
6 medium new potatoes, halved
2 tablespoons finely chopped fresh chives, to garnish

PREPARATION TIME: 25 minutes
COOKING TIME: 2 hours

1 Heat the oil in a large flameproof casserole over a moderate heat. Add the veal then, turning the pieces frequently, brown for 10 minutes. Sprinkle the flour over the meat. Continue cooking, stirring frequently, for 5 minutes, until the flour is brown.

2 Add the garlic to the casserole and cook for 30 seconds. Pour the stock into the casserole and stir well to combine. Add the tomato purée, parsley, thyme, bay leaf, salt and pepper. Cover and simmer over a medium-low heat for 30 minutes.

3 Melt the butter in a large frying pan over a medium heat. Add the onions and carrots, then cook for 5 minutes, stirring frequently. Sprinkle with the sugar and cook for 5 minutes, stirring constantly. Transfer the vegetables with a slotted spoon to the veal mixture. Cover and cook for 30 minutes.

4 Add the potatoes to the casserole. Cover and cook for 30 minutes. [A]

5 Taste the casserole and adjust the seasoning, if necessary. Sprinkle with the chives and serve immediately.

[A] The casserole may be prepared up to a day in advance, covered and kept chilled. Reheat for 20 minutes over a medium heat until hot before continuing with the recipe.

BAKED BEAN CASSEROLE

SERVES 6

4 slices streaky bacon, rinded
2 medium onions, peeled and finely chopped
2 green peppers, cored, seeded and chopped
2 × 450 g (1 lb) cans baked beans in tomato sauce
8 frankfurters, cut into 5 cm (2 inch) lengths
2 tablespoons demerara sugar
1 tablespoon Worcestershire sauce
1 teaspoon prepared mustard
salt
freshly ground black pepper

PREPARATION TIME: 20 minutes
COOKING TIME: 45 minutes
OVEN: 160°C, 325°F, Gas Mark 3

1 Place the bacon in a large frying pan over a moderate heat. Cook, turning frequently, until crisp. Drain on paper towels, then crumble the bacon. Set aside.

2 Heat the bacon drippings in the frying pan over a moderate heat. Add the onions and green peppers. Cook for 5 minutes, stirring frequently. Remove the pan from the heat.

3 Combine the bacon, onions, green peppers, baked beans, frankfurters, sugar, Worcestershire sauce, mustard, salt and pepper in a large bowl. Stir well. Transfer the mixture to a medium casserole. Place the casserole uncovered in a preheated oven and cook for 30 minutes, until heated through.

4 Serve the casserole with toast and a cooked green vegetable.

SWEDISH MEATBALLS

SERVES 6–8
15 g (½ oz) butter
1 medium onion, peeled and finely chopped
2 eggs, beaten
50 ml (2 fl oz) milk
100 g (4 oz) soft breadcrumbs
450 g (1 lb) minced beef
100 g (4 oz) minced pork
1 teaspoon dried dillweed
¾ teaspoon ground allspice
¼ teaspoon ground nutmeg
⅛ teaspoon ground cardamom
salt
freshly ground black pepper
5 tablespoons vegetable oil
3 tablespoons plain flour
600 ml (1 pint) beef stock
120 ml (4 fl oz) double or whipping cream
sprig fresh dill, to garnish

PREPARATION TIME: 25 minutes, plus
chilling
COOKING TIME: 55 minutes
OVEN: 160°C, 325°F, Gas Mark 3

1 Melt the butter in a medium frying pan over a moderate heat. Add the onion and, stirring frequently, cook for 10 minutes or until soft and golden. Remove the pan from the heat.

2 Combine the eggs, milk and breadcrumbs in a large bowl. Add the cooked onions. Blend in the beef, pork, ½ teaspoon of the dillweed, allspice, nutmeg, cardamom, salt and pepper. Cover and chill for 1 hour.

3 Shape the meat into 2.5 cm (1 inch) balls [A]. Heat the oil in a frying pan over a moderate heat. Brown the meatballs for 10 minutes. Transfer the meatballs with a slotted spoon to a large casserole.

4 Add the flour to the frying pan. Cook for 2–3 minutes, stirring constantly. Lower the heat. Blend in the beef stock, cream, remaining dillweed, salt and pepper. Cook for 5 minutes. When the sauce is smooth and thick, pour over the meatballs. Cover the casserole and place in a preheated oven. Cook for 30 minutes.

5 To serve, garnish the casserole with the dill. Serve with buttered noodles.

[A] The meatballs may be made earlier in the day, covered and kept chilled.

From the top: Veal Ragoût; Baked Bean Casserole; Swedish Meatballs

GINGERED POT ROAST

TO MARINATE:

1 kg (2¼ lb) brisket, tied
1 teaspoon ground ginger
2 teaspoons salt
freshly ground black pepper
350 ml (12 fl oz) dry red wine
4 tablespoons red wine vinegar
4 tablespoons water
1 small onion, peeled and thinly sliced
1 small carrot, peeled and thinly sliced
1 tablespoon finely chopped fresh parsley
1 tablespoon finely chopped fresh tarragon or ½
teaspoon dried tarragon
2 bay leaves, crushed
2 cloves

TO COOK:

4 tablespoons vegetable oil
1.2 litres (2 pints) beef stock
2 tablespoons brandy
1 garlic clove, peeled and finely chopped
1 bay leaf
8 small carrots, peeled
8 small onions, peeled
4 medium potatoes, peeled and quartered
100 g (4 oz) button mushrooms, cleaned
and skinned, if necessary

TO FINISH:

6 tablespoons cornflour
120 ml (4 fl oz) beef stock
1 teaspoon ground ginger

From left: Gingered Pot Roast; Stuffed Cabbage Rolls

PREPARATION TIME: 45 minutes, plus
marinating overnight
COOKING TIME: 4 hours

1 Rub the meat thoroughly with the ginger, salt and pepper. Place in a deep glass bowl.

2 Combine the remaining ingredients for the marinade in a large bowl. Pour over the meat and cover. Chill for 8 hours, turning the meat frequently. [A]

3 Remove the meat from the marinade and pat dry with paper towels. Strain the marinade and reserve.

4 Heat the oil in a large flameproof casserole over a medium-high heat. Add the meat and brown on all sides, turning frequently. Add the marinade, stock, brandy, garlic and bay leaf. Bring to the boil. Cover and reduce the heat to low. Simmer gently for 3 hours, skimming when necessary. Turn the meat at least once.

5 Add the carrots, onions, potatoes and mushrooms to the casserole. Cover and simmer for 40 minutes.

6 Transfer the meat and vegetables to a heated serving platter, removing the string from the meat, and keep warm. Skim the fat from the sauce. Place the casserole over a high heat and bring to the boil. Using a whisk, combine the cornflour, stock and ginger in a medium bowl until smooth. Pour the cornflour mixture into

the casserole and simmer until thick and smooth, stirring constantly. Taste the sauce and correct the seasoning, if necessary.

7 To serve, moisten the meat and vegetables with a little sauce – and serve the remaining sauce separately in a sauceboat.

[A] The meat may be marinated for up to 3 days, turning frequently.

STUFFED CABBAGE ROLLS

SERVES 8

FOR THE SAUCE:
25 g (1 oz) butter
1 carrot, peeled and diced
1 leek, white part only, thinly sliced
1 stick celery, thinly sliced
2 tablespoons plain flour
750 ml (1¼ pints) beef stock
1 tablespoon tomato purée
1 tablespoon fresh thyme leaves or ½ teaspoon dried thyme
1 bay leaf
salt
freshly ground black pepper

FOR THE STUFFING:
4.25 litres (8 pints) water
1 × 1 kg (2 lb) green cabbage, cored
175 g (6 oz) streaky bacon, rinded and cut into thin strips
750 g (1½ lb) minced beef
1 medium onion, peeled and finely chopped
2 garlic cloves, peeled and finely chopped
2 eggs, beaten
salt
freshly ground black pepper

TO COOK:
250 g (9 oz) streaky bacon, rinded and cut into thin strips
3 large tomatoes, peeled and diced
2 carrots, peeled and thinly sliced
1 large onion, peeled and thinly sliced
1 tablespoon fresh thyme or ½ teaspoon dried thyme
2 bay leaves, crushed

PREPARATION TIME: 45 minutes
COOKING TIME: 2 hours
OVEN: 190°C, 375°F, Gas Mark 5

Cabbage rolls are a favourite among middle Europeans. They make an inexpensive dish good for casual entertaining. This recipe can be made the day before and reheated, covered, at 190°C, 375°F, Gas Mark 5 for 30 minutes.

1 For the sauce, melt the butter in a medium saucepan over a moderate heat. Add the carrot, leek and celery. Cook for 5 minutes, stirring frequently. Blend in the flour and cook for 2–3 minutes, stirring constantly. Using a whisk, gradually stir in the stock, tomato purée, thyme, bay leaf, salt and pepper. Bring the mixture to the boil, stirring frequently. Lower the heat, then simmer gently for 30 minutes, removing the scum frequently. Remove the sauce from the heat and strain. Set aside. [A]

2 For the stuffing, bring the water to the boil in a large saucepan. Using a large metal strainer, dip the cabbage carefully in the water. Remove after 30 seconds. Remove the 3 or 4 leaves which have now been loosened. Dip the cabbage carefully again in the water for 30 seconds. Remove the loosened leaves. Continue dipping and removing the leaves until you have 16 leaves. Return the leaves to the boiling water and cook for 2 minutes. Drain immediately under cold running water, then set aside.

3 Place the bacon in a large frying pan over a moderate heat. Cook for 5 minutes, stirring frequently. Add the mince, onion and garlic. Continue cooking for 10 minutes, until the meat is no longer pink and the onion is tender. Drain off the excess fat and discard. Transfer the mixture to a large heatproof bowl. Stir in the eggs, salt and pepper. Mix thoroughly. [A]

4 To stuff the cabbage rolls, place the leaves flat on a working surface. For each roll, place 50 g (2 oz) of the stuffing at the base or stem-end of each cabbage leaf. Fold in the sides, then roll the cabbage away from you to completely enclose the filling. Repeat for the remaining rolls.

5 To cook, place the bacon slices in a large casserole. Sprinkle the remaining ingredients evenly over the bacon. Place the cabbage rolls, seam side down and touching each other, in layers on the vegetable base. Cover tightly with aluminium foil and the casserole lid. [A] Place in a preheated oven and cook for 30 minutes.

6 Remove the foil from the casserole. Pour the sauce over the cabbage rolls, making sure to coat all the rolls. Return to the oven and cook uncovered for 20–30 minutes.

7 To serve, transfer the cabbage rolls to a heated serving platter, with the bacon slices, if liked. Taste the sauce and adjust the seasoning, if necessary. Pour the sauce over the rolls.

[A] Can be prepared several hours in advance, covered and kept chilled.

STUFFED GREEN PEPPERS

FOR THE TOMATO SAUCE:
2 × 400 g (14 oz) cans tomatoes
1 medium onion, peeled and studded with 4 cloves
2 celery sticks, chopped
1 carrot, peeled and diced
4 parsley sprigs
1 sprig fresh thyme or ¼ teaspoon dried thyme
1 bay leaf
40 g (1½ oz) butter
2 tablespoons plain flour
½ teaspoon sugar
1 tablespoon finely chopped fresh basil or ½ teaspoon dried basil

FOR THE PEPPERS:
4 large green peppers
2.75 litres (5 pints) water
225 g (8 oz) minced beef
1 small onion, peeled and finely chopped
400 g (14 oz) cooked rice
4 tablespoons finely chopped fresh parsley
½ teaspoon dried mixed herbs
salt
freshly ground black pepper
2 eggs, beaten

PREPARATION TIME: 20 minutes
COOKING TIME: 2 hours
OVEN: 180°C, 350°F, Gas Mark 4

1 For the tomato sauce, combine the tomatoes, onion, celery, carrot, parsley, thyme and bay leaf in a medium saucepan. Bring to the boil over a high heat. Reduce the heat to medium-low, then cover and simmer for 30 minutes.

2 Strain the sauce through a sieve, pressing hard on the vegetables. Set aside.

3 Melt the butter in a medium saucepan over a moderate heat. Blend in the flour and cook for 2–3 minutes, stirring constantly. Using a whisk, gradually stir in the strained tomato sauce. Add the sugar and basil. Bring the mixture to a simmer and cook for 10 minutes. Remove from the heat and set aside. [A]

4 For the peppers, cut off the tops of the peppers and discard. Carefully remove the core and seeds and discard.

5 Bring the water to the boil in a large saucepan. Add the peppers and cook for 5 minutes. Drain well, then rinse under cold running water. Set the peppers aside.

6 Place the mince and onion in a large saucepan. Cook over a moderate heat for 10 minutes until the meat is no longer pink and the onion is tender. Remove the pan from the heat and, if necessary, drain off the fat. Stir in the rice, parsley, mixed herbs, salt and pepper. Blend in the eggs. [A]

7 Fill the peppers evenly with the meat mixture. Place the peppers, standing upright, in a medium casserole. Add the tomato sauce to the casserole, spooning a small amount of the sauce over each pepper. Cover and place the casserole in a preheated oven. Cook for 30 minutes.

8 Serve immediately with a cucumber and dill salad.

[A] The tomato sauce and filling may be prepared several hours in advance, covered and kept chilled.

BEEF ROULADEN

SERVES 6
6 × 150 g (5 oz) slices of topside or silverside of beef
1 tablespoon Dijon mustard
salt
freshly ground black pepper
1 medium onion, peeled and finely chopped
1½ dill pickles, cut lengthwise into quarters
1 tablespoon vegetable oil
15 g (½ oz) butter
100 g (4 oz) button mushrooms, cleaned and sliced
450 ml (¾ pint) beef stock
120 ml (4 fl oz) dry red wine
1½ tablespoons cornflour
2 tablespoons finely chopped fresh parsley, to garnish

PREPARATION TIME: 20 minutes
COOKING TIME: 1¾ hours
OVEN: 180°C, 350°F, Gas Mark 4

Beef Rouladen, using these thin slices of topside of beef, are a German speciality. The piquancy of the mustard and dill pickles is a good counterpoint against the relative blandness of the meat. Make sure that the beef slices are pounded very thinly by your butcher, otherwise they will be difficult to roll up into neat 'olives', as we call them.

1 Spread the beef slices evenly with the mustard. Season with the salt and pepper. Sprinkle the onion evenly over each slice. Top with 1 dill pickle quarter. Roll each beef slice up and secure with wooden toothpicks. [A]

2 Heat the oil and butter in a flameproof casserole over a moderate heat. Add the beef rouladen and, turning frequently, brown on all

Top: Stuffed Green Peppers, bottom: Beef Rouladen

sides for 10 minutes. Add the mushrooms, 350 ml (12 fl oz) of the stock and the wine. Reduce the heat to low, then cover. Place in a preheated oven and cook for 1¼ hours.

3 Transfer the rouladen to a heated serving platter and keep warm. Bring the sauce to the boil over a high heat. Combine the cornflour and remaining stock in a cup until smooth. Using a whisk, blend the cornflour mixture into the sauce. Cook for 2-3 minutes, until the sauce is smooth and has thickened.

4 To serve, pour the sauce over the rouladen and sprinkle with the parsley. Serve with boiled potatoes, red cabbage and a cucumber and soured cream salad.

[A] Can be prepared earlier in the day, covered and kept chilled.

BRAISED ITALIAN HUNTER'S CHICKEN

SERVES 8

25 g (1 oz) dried Italian (or porcini) mushrooms
350 ml (12 fl oz) warm water
50 ml (2 fl oz) olive oil
2 × 1½ kg (3 lb) chickens, each cut into 8 serving
pieces
2 leeks, white part only, sliced
1 large onion, peeled and chopped
75 g (3 oz) unsmoked ham, cubed
2 garlic cloves, peeled and finely chopped
1 tablespoon finely chopped fresh marjoram or
½ teaspoon dried marjoram
1 tablespoon finely chopped fresh rosemary or
½ teaspoon dried rosemary
¾ teaspoon fresh thyme or ¼ teaspoon dried thyme
½ teaspoon finely chopped fresh savory or
⅛ teaspoon dried savory
400 ml (14 fl oz) chicken stock
120 ml (4 fl oz) dry red wine
1 tablespoon tomato purée
salt
freshly ground black pepper
2 tablespoons cornflour
50 ml (2 fl oz) red wine

PREPARATION TIME: 20 minutes, plus
soaking
COOKING TIME: 55 minutes

1 Soak the mushrooms in the water for 30 minutes. Drain the mushrooms, reserving the soaking liquid. Chop the mushrooms and set aside. Strain and retain the liquid.

2 Heat the oil in a large flameproof casserole over a medium-high heat. Place the chicken, skin side down, in the casserole. Brown for 10 minutes, turning occasionally. Remove the chicken from the casserole with tongs or a slotted spoon and set aside.

3 Add the leeks and onion to the casserole. Cook for 5 minutes, stirring occasionally. Add the ham, garlic, marjoram, rosemary, thyme and savory. Cook for 1 minute. Stir in the reserved mushrooms and soaking liquid, the stock, wine, tomato purée, salt and pepper.

4 Season the chicken with the salt and pepper. Return to the casserole. Cover and cook over a medium-low heat for 25 minutes. Remove the breast pieces from the casserole and keep warm on a heated serving platter. Continue cooking the dark meat pieces for another 10 minutes then remove them to the serving platter. [A]

5 Skim the fat off the sauce thoroughly, then

bring it to the boil. Combine the cornflour and red wine in a cup until smooth. Using a whisk, blend into the sauce. Simmer for 2–3 minutes, until thick and smooth. To serve, pour the sauce over the chicken pieces.

[A] Can be prepared the day before, covered and kept chilled. Cook over a medium-low heat until the chicken is hot before continuing with the recipe.

CHICKEN AND SAUSAGE CASSEROLE WITH DUMPLINGS

3 × 400 g (14 oz) can tomatoes
2 teaspoons sugar
1 × 1¼ kg (2½ lb) chicken, cut into 8 pieces
salt
freshly ground black pepper
1 tablespoon olive oil
450 g (1 lb) uncooked Italian sausages, pricked
1 large onion, peeled and chopped
100 g (4 oz) button mushrooms, cleaned and sliced
1 green pepper, cored, seeded and cubed
1 garlic clove, peeled and finely chopped
120 ml (4 fl oz) chicken stock
120 ml (4 fl oz) dry white wine
2 tablespoons finely chopped fresh oregano

FOR THE TOPPING:
50 g (2 oz) self-raising flour
50 g (2 oz) soft white breadcrumbs
2 tablespoons shredded suet
1 tablespoon finely chopped fresh parsley
2 teaspoons finely grated lemon rind
salt
freshly ground white pepper
1 egg, beaten

PREPARATION TIME: 40 minutes
COOKING TIME: 50 minutes
OVEN: 200°C, 400°F, Gas Mark 6

1 Place the tomatoes in a saucepan over a medium-high heat. Cook for 20 minutes, stirring occasionally, until reduced to 475 ml (16 fl oz). Stir in the sugar, then set aside.

2 Season the chicken pieces with the salt and pepper. Heat the oil in a large flameproof casserole over a medium-high heat. Add the chicken, skin side down, and the sausages. Cook for 10 minutes, turning frequently, until brown. Drain off the excess fat and discard.

3 Add the tomatoes, onion, mushrooms, green pepper, garlic, stock, wine, oregano, salt and pepper. Stir well to incorporate all the bits. Bring the sauce to the boil, cover the casserole

and cook in a preheated oven for 25 minutes.

4 To make the topping, mix together the flour, breadcrumbs, suet, parsley, lemon rind, salt and pepper in a large bowl. Make a well in the centre of the mixture, then place the egg in the well. Drawing in the flour mixture from the sides, quickly combine the dough. Shape the mixture into 8 balls.

5 Place the balls on the casserole. Cover and transfer to a preheated oven. Cook for 20 minutes or until the topping is cooked.

STOVED CHICKEN

50 g (2 oz) flour
salt
freshly ground black pepper
1 × 1½ kg (3½ lb) chicken, cut into 8 pieces
50 g (2 oz) butter
1¼ kg (2½ lb) potatoes, peeled and thinly sliced
25 g (1 oz) melted butter
1 large onion, peeled and thinly sliced
600 ml (1 pint) chicken stock
2 tablespoons chopped fresh parsley, to garnish

PREPARATION TIME: 30 minutes
COOKING TIME: 2¼ hours
OVEN: 150°C, 300°F, Gas Mark 2

1 Combine the flour, salt and pepper and coat the chicken pieces in the mixture.

2 Melt the butter in a large flameproof casserole over a moderate heat. Add the chicken pieces and brown for 10 minutes, turning frequently. Transfer the chicken pieces to a plate. Remove the casserole from the heat.

3 Arrange ⅓ of the potato slices in the casserole. Brush with ⅓ of the melted butter. Season with the salt and pepper. Arrange ½ of the onion slices on the potatoes. Place 4 of the chicken pieces on the onions. Arrange ⅓ of the potato slices over the chicken pieces. Brush with ⅓ of the melted butter, then season. Repeat the onion, chicken and potato layers. Brush with the remaining butter, then season. Pour the stock over to just cover the potatoes. Cover with greased greaseproof paper and the casserole lid. [A] Cook in a preheated oven for 2 hours. [A]

4 Uncover the casserole and continue to cook for 30 minutes. Garnish with the parsley.

[A] Can be prepared earlier in the day, either before or after the 2 hours' cooking.

From the top: Braised Italian Hunter's Chicken; Chicken and Sausage Casserole with Dumplings; Stoved Chicken

BRAISED CHICKEN WITH NEW POTATOES AND PAPRIKA

2 tablespoons vegetable oil
200 g (7 oz) streaky bacon, rinded and cut into strips
1 × 1½ kg (3 lb) chicken, cut into 8 pieces
salt
freshly ground black pepper
1 large onion, peeled and chopped
1 large green pepper, cored, seeded and chopped
1 garlic clove, peeled and finely chopped
2 tablespoons plain flour
2 tablespoons sweet Hungarian paprika
600 ml (1 pint) chicken stock
120 ml (4 fl oz) dry white wine
12 small red or white new potatoes, halved
300 ml (½ pint) soured cream
2 tablespoons plain flour

PREPARATION TIME: 25 minutes
COOKING TIME: 1¼ hours

Sweet Hungarian paprika, for which there is no real substitute, is available in delicatessens or the speciality sections of supermarkets. It should be stored in the fridge or freezer to retain its bold flavour.

1 Heat the oil in a large flameproof casserole over a moderate heat. Add the bacon and cook for 5 minutes, stirring frequently. Remove the bacon with a slotted spoon and set aside. Pour off all but 3 tablespoons of the fat.

2 Season the chicken pieces with the salt and pepper. Place in the casserole, skin side down, over a medium-high heat. Brown, turning occasionally, for 10–15 minutes. Remove the chicken with tongs and set aside.

3 Place the onion in the casserole over a medium heat. Cook, stirring occasionally, for 5 minutes. Add the pepper and garlic, then cook for 1 minute. Blend in the flour and paprika and cook for 2–3 minutes, stirring constantly. Using a whisk, gradually blend in the stock and wine. Bring the mixture to the boil and cook until the sauce is smooth and thick.

4 Return the chicken and bacon to the sauce. Arrange the potatoes around the chicken. Cover and cook over a medium-low heat for 30 minutes. Remove the breast pieces from the casserole and keep warm on a heated serving platter. Continue cooking the dark meat pieces for another 10 minutes.

5 Remove the remaining chicken pieces and place on the serving platter. Keep warm. Test the potatoes. If they are not tender, cover the casserole and cook over a medium-low heat until they are cooked. Remove the potatoes with a slotted spoon and arrange around the chicken pieces. [A]

6 To finish the sauce, reduce the heat to very low. Combine the soured cream and flour in a small bowl until smooth. Using a whisk, stir into the sauce. Cook gently for 2 minutes.

7 Pour the sauce over the chicken and potatoes. Serve with noodles and a green vegetable.

[A] Can be prepared the day before, then covered and kept chilled. Reheat gently for 20 minutes, before continuing with the recipe.

TURKEY HASH

SERVES 6
40 g (1½ oz) butter
1 medium onion, peeled and finely chopped
1 red pepper, cored, seeded and diced
225 g (8 oz) button mushrooms, cleaned and sliced
1 garlic clove, peeled and finely chopped
450 g (1 lb) cooked turkey meat, cubed
275 g (10 oz) leftover turkey stuffing, cubed
300 ml (½ pint) double or whipping cream
250 ml (8 fl oz) turkey or chicken stock
120 ml (4 fl oz) leftover turkey gravy
2 tablespoons cornflour
15 g (½ oz) finely chopped fresh parsley
⅛ teaspoon ground nutmeg
salt
freshly ground black pepper
25 g (1 oz) Gruyère cheese, grated

PREPARATION TIME: 25 minutes
COOKING TIME: 50 minutes
OVEN: 180°C, 350°F, Gas Mark 4

1 Melt the butter in a medium flameproof casserole over a moderate heat. Add the onion and cook, stirring frequently, for 5 minutes. Add the pepper, mushrooms and garlic. Cook for 3 minutes, until the mushrooms begin to soften. Add the turkey and stuffing, then cook for 5 minutes, stirring occasionally. Remove the casserole from the heat and set aside.

2 Combine the cream, 175 ml (6 fl oz) of the stock and the gravy in a medium saucepan. Bring to the boil over a high heat. Combine the cornflour and the remaining stock in a cup until smooth and, using a whisk, stir into the sauce. Simmer for 2–3 minutes, stirring constantly, until smooth and thick. Remove from the heat and add the parsley, nutmeg, salt and pepper. Blend the sauce into the casserole, then sprinkle over the cheese. [A] Cover the casserole, place in a preheated oven and cook for 25 minutes until heated through.

3 Serve with crisp toast and a green salad.

[A] The casserole can be prepared in the morning, covered and kept chilled. Cook for 30 minutes until heated through.

SOMERSET CHICKEN

4 tablespoons plain flour
salt
freshly ground black pepper
4 boneless chicken breasts, about 150 g (5 oz) each,
skinned and cut into bite-sized pieces
1 medium onion, peeled and finely chopped
175 g (6 oz) button mushrooms, cleaned and sliced
2 tablespoons finely chopped fresh parsley
2 teaspoons mixed dried herbs
1 kg (2 lb) potatoes, peeled and thinly sliced
300 ml (½ pint) chicken stock
300 ml (½ pint) dry cider
chopped fresh parsley, to garnish

PREPARATION TIME: 25 minutes
COOKING TIME: 1¼ hours
OVEN: 190°C, 375°F, Gas Mark 5

1 Place the flour, salt and pepper in a plastic bag. Add the chicken pieces and tightly seal the opening of the bag. Shake well to coat the chicken thoroughly. Transfer the chicken pieces to a large casserole.

2 Add the onion, mushrooms, parsley, herbs, salt and pepper to the casserole.

3 Arrange the potatoes on the top of the casserole. Pour in the chicken stock and cider. The potatoes should just be covered with liquid. [A] Cover the casserole and place in a preheated oven. Cook for 1 hour.

4 Take the lid off the casserole and cook for 15 minutes, until the top is brown.

5 Garnish with the parsley and serve with a green vegetable.

[A] Can be prepared several hours in advance, covered and kept chilled.

Clockwise from top left: Turkey Hash; Braised Chicken with New Potatoes and Paprika; Somerset Chicken

SHANK END OF LAMB WITH LEMON-DILL SAUCE

*4 slices from a shank end of lamb, about 225 g (8 oz)
each
2 garlic cloves, peeled and cut into 16 thin slices each
50 g (2 oz) plain flour
salt
freshly ground black pepper
25 ml (1 fl oz) vegetable oil
1 medium onion, peeled and thinly sliced
2 sticks celery, thinly sliced
1 tablespoon fresh thyme leaves or ½ teaspoon dried
thyme
1 × 5 cm (2 inch) piece of lemon peel
1 bay leaf
450 ml (¾ pint) chicken or lamb stock
3 eggs, beaten
85 ml (3 fl oz) lemon juice
3 tablespoons finely chopped fresh dill or 2 teaspoons
dried dillweed*

PREPARATION TIME: 20 minutes
COOKING TIME: 1½ hours
OVEN: 160°C, 325°F, Gas Mark 3

1 Make 8 small incisions in the meaty part of each shank piece. Insert 1 garlic slice into each incision.

2 Combine the flour, salt and pepper on a large plate. Coat the lamb thoroughly in the flour, then shake off the excess.

3 Heat the oil in a large flameproof casserole over a medium-high heat. Add the lamb and brown for 10 minutes, turning frequently. Transfer the meat with a slotted spoon to a plate and set aside.

4 Add the onion, celery, thyme, lemon peel and bay leaf to the casserole. Cook over a moderate heat for 5 minutes until the vegetables have softened. Blend in the stock and bring the mixture to the boil. Add the shank pieces to the casserole, then cover and place in a preheated oven. Cook for 1 hour, or until they are tender. [A]

5 Transfer the lamb to a heated serving platter and keep warm. Strain the cooking liquid through a sieve into a medium saucepan. Skim the fat. Reduce the liquid over a high heat to 250 ml (8 fl oz).

6 Combine the eggs and lemon juice in a large bowl. Using a whisk, gradually stir the hot liquid into the egg mixture. Return the mixture to the saucepan and cook over a low heat, stirring constantly, until it is thick and smooth. Do not boil. Add the dill, salt and pepper.

7 Pour the sauce over the lamb and serve immediately. Orzo (rice-shaped pasta) or rice are natural accompaniments.

[A] Can be prepared the day before, covered and kept chilled. Reheat over a moderate heat for 15–20 minutes until the meat is hot before continuing with the recipe.

BRAISED SHANK END OF LAMB WITH A BOUQUET OF VEGETABLES

*4 pieces of shank end (or knuckle) of lamb,
about 350 g (12 oz) each
1 tablespoon fresh thyme or ½ teaspoon dried thyme
salt
freshly ground black pepper
50 g (2 oz) butter
2 tablespoons oil
1 medium onion, peeled and finely chopped
600 ml (1 pint) dry white wine
600 ml (1 pint) chicken or lamb stock
2 medium carrots, peeled and diced
2 sticks celery, diced
100 g (4 oz) thawed frozen peas or cooked fresh peas*

*TO FINISH:
4 tablespoons cornflour
50 ml (2 fl oz) dry white wine
1 tablespoon finely chopped parsley, to garnish*

PREPARATION TIME: 20 minutes
COOKING TIME: 2¼ hours
OVEN: 160°C, 325°F, Gas Mark 3

1 Sprinkle the lamb with the thyme, salt and pepper. Heat the butter and oil in a large flameproof casserole. Add the lamb and onion. Cook, turning frequently, for 10 minutes until the shanks are brown.

2 Add the wine and stock to the casserole. Place in a preheated oven. Cook for 1½ hours, until tender. Cover the casserole if the liquid reduces too quickly. [A]

3 Remove the lamb from the casserole and cut the meat from the bone into bite-sized pieces. Set aside.

4 Skim the fat from the liquid. Add the meat, carrots and celery. Cook over a medium–high heat for 15 minutes, stirring occasionally.

5 Combine the cornflour and white wine in a cup until smooth. Using a whisk, stir into the casserole. Cook, stirring constantly, until smooth and thick.

6 Add the peas to the meat mixture. Cook for 3–4 minutes.

7 To serve, transfer the casserole to a heated serving platter. Sprinkle with the parsley and serve immediately.

[A] Can be prepared the day before, covered and kept chilled. Simmer over a medium heat for 20 minutes before continuing with the recipe.

From the left: Shank End of Lamb with Lemon Dill Sauce; Braised Shank End of Lamb with a Bouquet of Vegetables

COD AND CHEDDAR CASSEROLE

50 g (2 oz) butter
1 medium onion, peeled and finely chopped
100 g (4 oz) button mushrooms, cleaned and sliced
50 g (2 oz) plain flour
350 ml (12 fl oz) milk
50 ml (2 fl oz) dry white wine
175 g (6 oz) Cheddar cheese, grated
salt
freshly ground white pepper
750 g (1½ lb) thick cod or haddock fillets, skinned
1 red pepper, cored, seeded and diced

FOR THE TOPPING:
50 g (2 oz) self-raising flour
50 g (2 oz) soft white breadcrumbs
2 tablespoons shredded suet
1 tablespoon finely chopped fresh parsley
2 teaspoons finely grated lemon rind
salt
freshly ground white pepper
1 egg, beaten

PREPARATION TIME: 45 minutes
COOKING TIME: 1 hour
OVEN: 200°C, 400°F, Gas Mark 6

1 Melt the butter in a large saucepan over a moderate heat. Add the onion and mushrooms, then cook for 10 minutes, stirring occasionally. Blend in the flour and cook for 2–3 minutes, stirring frequently. Using a whisk, gradually stir in the milk and white wine. Bring the sauce to the boil and simmer for 2–3 minutes until smooth and thick. Add the cheese, salt and pepper and cook until the cheese has just melted. Remove the sauce from the heat and set aside.

2 Place the cod fillets in a large casserole. Sprinkle with the red pepper. Pour the sauce over the cod. Set aside.

3 To make the topping, mix together the flour, breadcrumbs, suet, parsley, lemon rind, salt and pepper in a large bowl. Make a well in the centre of the mixture, then place the egg in the well. Drawing in the flour mixture from the sides, quickly combine the dough. Shape the mixture into 8 balls.

4 Place the balls on the casserole. Cover and cook for 20 minutes or until the topping is cooked and the fish flakes easily.

From the top: Cod and Cheddar Casserole; Haddock with Cider and Vegetables; Prawn, Garlic and Herb Casserole

HADDOCK WITH CIDER AND VEGETABLES

250 ml (8 fl oz) dry cider
2 medium onions, peeled and thinly sliced
750 g (1½ lb) boneless and skinned haddock fillets,
cut into 10 cm (4 inch) pieces
1 green pepper, cored, seeded and diced
3 medium tomatoes, peeled, seeded and chopped
1 tablespoon finely chopped fresh parsley
1 tablespoon finely chopped fresh marjoram or
1 teaspoon dried marjoram
salt
freshly ground black pepper
4 tablespoons fresh white breadcrumbs
25 g (1 oz) freshly grated Parmesan cheese

TO GARNISH:
2 lemon wedges
1 large sprig parsley

PREPARATION TIME: 30 minutes
COOKING TIME: 30 minutes
OVEN: 160°C, 325°F, Gas Mark 3

1 Place the cider in a medium saucepan over a high heat. Bring to the boil, then reduce the heat to medium. Add the onions. Simmer for 5 minutes, or until the cider has reduced by a quarter. Remove the mixture from the heat.

2 Place the fish in a flameproof casserole. Stir in the cider mixture, green pepper, tomatoes, parsley, marjoram, salt and pepper. Cover the casserole and bring to the boil over a high heat. Place in a preheated oven and cook for 15 minutes, or until the fish flakes easily.

3 Combine the breadcrumbs and cheese together in a small bowl. Remove the casserole from the oven and sprinkle with the breadcrumb mixture. Place under a preheated grill and cook for 2–3 minutes, until browned. Garnish with the lemon wedges and parsley sprigs, then serve immediately.

PRAWN, GARLIC AND HERB CASSEROLE

120 ml (4 fl oz) olive oil
120 ml (4 fl oz) dry white vermouth or dry white
wine
85 ml (3 fl oz) lemon juice
4 garlic cloves, peeled and finely chopped
15 g (½ oz) finely chopped fresh parsley
2½ tablespoons finely chopped fresh oregano or
1½ teaspoons dried oregano
salt
freshly ground black pepper
750 g (1½ lb) prawns, peeled, deveined and tails left
intact

TO GARNISH:
4 lemon twists
4 sprigs parsley

PREPARATION TIME: 30 minutes, plus cooling and marinating
COOKING TIME: 30 minutes
OVEN: 190°C, 375°F, Gas Mark 5

Prawns as an everyday meal? According to the season and market availability, the price of prawns does fluctuate. Freezer stores and supermarkets also occasionally have special prices for their prawns. Make your family feel pampered by serving prawns and make your purse feel good by paying a low price for the prawns.

1 Combine the oil, vermouth or wine, lemon juice, garlic, parsley, and oregano in a medium saucepan. Place over a medium-high heat and bring to the boil, stirring frequently. Remove from the heat and season to taste with the salt and pepper. Set aside and let cool for 30 minutes.

2 Arrange the prawns in a single layer in a flameproof casserole dish. Pour the vermouth mixture over the prawns. Cover with the casserole lid and marinate at room temperature for 1 hour.

3 Place the prawns, in the marinade, in a preheated oven. Cook for 10–15 minutes, or until pink and firm.

4 Remove the prawns from the casserole, arrange them on a heated serving platter and keep them warm. Place the cooking liquid over a high heat and reduce until thickened. Pour the sauce over the prawns, then garnish with the lemon twists and parsley sprigs.

FRENCH CAFÉ BEEF CASSEROLE

SERVES 4–6
25 ml (1 fl oz) vegetable oil
750 g (1½ lb) chuck steak, trimmed and cut into
2.5 cm (1 inch) cubes
1 large onion, peeled and thinly sliced
175 g (6 oz) button mushrooms, cleaned and
quartered
4 slices streaky bacon, rinded and chopped
1 × 225 g (8 oz) can tomatoes
175 ml (6 fl oz) beef stock
2 garlic cloves, peeled and finely chopped
1 teaspoon allspice
½ teaspoon dried mixed herbs
salt
freshly ground black pepper
2 tablespoons plain flour
85 ml (3 fl oz) dry red wine
50 g (2 oz) butter, softened
1 tablespoon wholegrain mustard
8 slices of French bread, cut diagonally in 1 cm
(½ inch) slices
1 sprig fresh parsley, to garnish

PREPARATION TIME: 30 minutes
COOKING TIME: 2½ hours
OVEN: 150°C, 300°F, Gas Mark 2

1 Heat the oil in a large flameproof casserole over a medium-high heat. Add the meat and brown for 5–10 minutes, stirring frequently. Remove the meat from the casserole with a slotted spoon and set aside.

2 Add the onion, mushrooms and bacon to the casserole. Cook for 10 minutes until the onion is tender and the bacon is crisp. Drain off the excess fat and discard.

3 Return the meat to the casserole. Blend in the tomatoes, stock, garlic, allspice, mixed herbs, salt and pepper. Combine the flour and red wine in a cup until smooth. Stir into the casserole. Cover and place in a preheated oven. Cook for 2 hours, until the meat is tender.

4 To finish, combine the butter with the mustard. Spread the mixture evenly on one side of each bread slice. Arrange the slices, overlapping and mustard side up, on the top of the casserole. Brown under a preheated grill. Garnish the casserole with the parsley sprig, then serve immediately.

CHICKEN AND BROCCOLI ROLL-UPS

SERVES 6
65 g (2½ oz) butter
6 × 150 g (5 oz) chicken thighs, boned and skinned
6 small fresh broccoli spears
250 ml (8 fl oz) boiling water
120 ml (4 fl oz) chicken stock
salt
2 small onions, peeled and thinly sliced
2 tablespoons plain flour
½ tablespoon finely chopped fresh basil or
¼ teaspoon dried basil
¼ teaspoon celery salt
freshly ground white pepper
120 ml (4 fl oz) milk
6 × 25 g (1 oz) slices Swiss cheese

PREPARATION TIME: 35 minutes
COOKING TIME: 1¼ hours
OVEN: 180°C, 350°F, Gas Mark 4

This dish only *seems* complicated. It's pretty enough to serve to guests, but it is also inexpensive enough for an everyday meal.

1 Melt 2 tablespoons of the butter in a large frying pan over a moderate heat. Add the chicken thighs and brown for 10 minutes, turning frequently. Remove the thighs with a pair of tongs and set aside.

2 Dip the broccoli spears in the boiling water for a few seconds, remove them with a pair of tongs and dip them into the chicken stock. Discard the water or reserve for another use. Sprinkle the spears with the salt, then set aside. Reserve the chicken stock.

3 Melt 2 tablespoons of the butter in a small saucepan over a moderate heat. Add the onions and cook for 5–10 minutes, stirring frequently, until tender. Sprinkle the onions with the flour,

basil, celery salt, salt and pepper. Cook for 2–3 minutes, stirring constantly. Using a whisk, gradually stir in the reserved chicken stock and the milk. Cook for 5 minutes, stirring constantly, until smooth and thickened. Set aside.

4 To assemble each roll-up, wrap 1 slice of the cheese around 1 broccoli spear. Wrap 1 thigh around the cheese and broccoli spear. Secure with a wooden toothpick or small metal skewer. Season each completed roll-up lightly with salt and pepper.

5 Grease a medium casserole with the remaining butter. Arrange the roll-ups in the casserole and pour the sauce over them. Cover the casserole, place in a preheated oven and cook for 20 minutes.

6 Uncover the casserole and continue to cook for another 20 minutes.

7 Serve immediately with creamed potatoes and a tomato salad.

Left: French Café Beef Casserole; right: Chicken and Broccoli Roll-Ups

BACON AND POTATO HOT POT

20 g (¾ oz) butter, for greasing
750 g (1½ lb) peeled potatoes, thickly sliced
salt
freshly ground black pepper
450 g (1 lb) thickly sliced smoked bacon, rinded
2 tablespoons chopped parsley
2 medium onions, peeled and thinly sliced
600 ml (1 pint) chicken stock

PREPARATION TIME: 35 minutes
COOKING TIME: 2 hours
OVEN: 120°C, 250°F, Gas Mark 1/2

1 Grease a large casserole dish with 1 table-spoon of the butter. Place ⅓ of the potato slices on the bottom of the dish. Add the salt and pepper. Top with ½ of the bacon. Sprinkle ½ of the parsley on the bacon. Add ½ of the onion slices. Season with salt and pepper. Place ⅓ of the potato slices over the onion. Add the salt and pepper. Repeat the layers with the remaining bacon, parsley and onion slices and put the remaining potatoes in an overlapping layer on top. Add the salt and pepper. Pour the stock into the casserole dish. Grease a sheet of greaseproof paper with the remaining butter. Cover the casserole dish with the paper, then the lid. [A] Place in a preheated oven and cook for 1½ hours.

2 Remove the lid and greaseproof paper from the casserole. Return the casserole to the oven and cook for 20–30 minutes, until the top is brown.

[A] Can be prepared several hours in advance, covered and kept chilled.

Top: Bacon and Potato Hot Pot; bottom: Braised Stuffed Pork Chops

BRAISED STUFFED PORK CHOPS

SERVES 6

6 pork chops, about 175 g (6 oz) each, 2.5 cm
(1 inch) thick and fat trimmed
salt
freshly ground black pepper
100 g (4 oz) dried breadcrumbs
1 small onion, peeled and finely chopped
1 stick celery, finely sliced
1 garlic clove, peeled and finely chopped
2 tablespoons finely chopped fresh parsley
1 egg, beaten
¼ teaspoon paprika
2 tablespoons vegetable oil
650 ml (22 fl oz) chicken stock
120 ml (4 fl oz) white wine
2 tablespoons cornflour
120 ml (4 fl oz) double or whipping cream
bunch watercress, to garnish

PREPARATION TIME: 25 minutes
COOKING TIME: 1¾ hours
OVEN: 180°C, 350°F, Gas Mark 4

1 Cut a pocket in the side of the pork chops for the stuffing. Do not cut all the way through. Sprinkle the chops with the salt and pepper, then set aside.

2 Combine the breadcrumbs, onion, celery, garlic, parsley, egg, paprika, salt and pepper in a medium bowl. Stuff the pork chops with this mixture. Use metal skewers or wooden toothpicks to enclose the stuffing. Set aside.

3 Heat the oil in a flameproof casserole over a medium-high heat. Add the pork chops and brown on one side for 6–7 minutes. Turn the chops over and brown the other side for 4–5 minutes. Remove the chops from the casserole with tongs or a slotted spoon and set aside. Drain the excess fat from the casserole and discard.

4 Add 600 ml (1 pint) of the stock and the wine to the casserole, scraping the bottom to incorporate all the bits. When the stock mixture comes to the boil, return the pork chops to the casserole. Cover and place in a preheated oven. Cook for 1¼ hours. [A]

5 Remove the casserole from the oven. Transfer the chops to a heated serving platter and keep warm. Place the casserole over a high heat. Combine the cornflour and the remaining stock in a cup, stirring until smooth. Using a whisk, blend into the casserole. Bring to the boil, stirring constantly. Stir the cream into the casserole. Taste and adjust the seasoning, if necessary.

6 To serve, pour the sauce over the chops, then garnish with the watercress. Creamed potatoes, buttered green beans and apple sauce would go well with this dish.

Stuffing variations: For *prune stuffing*, omit the garlic and paprika. Soak 6 prunes in enough water to cover for 1 hour. Drain, stone and chop the prunes. Add them and ¼ teaspoon crumbled dried rosemary to the stuffing.

For *apple stuffing*, one small cooking apple, cored and finely chopped, and 50 g (2 oz) raisins may be added to the original stuffing.

For *sausage stuffing,* crumble 100 g (4 oz) sausage meat into a small frying pan and cook for 10 minutes, stirring frequently to break up the pieces, until browned and cooked through. Drain off any excess fat and add the sausage meat to the original stuffing.

With both the apple and sausage stuffings, any leftover stuffing can be placed in a small oven-proof dish and cooked for 20 minutes alongside the pork chops.

[A] Can be prepared several hours in advance, covered and kept chilled. Reheat gently over a low heat until the chops are hot before continuing with the recipe.

QUICK CASSEROLES

In this chapter the casserole dish becomes the
ideal medium for cooking sustaining meals in a
short time. Most of the recipes take only an hour
to cook and many can be both prepared and
cooked in that time. The secret lies in the clever
combining of smaller and more tender cuts of fresh
meats, poultry and fish or of cooked meats and
storecupboard standbys with pasta, rice or
vegetables. Some of the casseroles – Chicken,
Tomato and Olive Casserole and Gingered
Citrus Chicken, for instance – have sophisticated
flavours imparted by the more exotic herbs and
spices; others, like the Sausage and Apple
Casserole or the Frankfurter and Vegetable
Casserole should find favour with younger
members of the family.

MUSHROOM AND NOODLE CASSEROLE

SERVES 8
2.75 litres (5 pints) water
350 g (12 oz) fettucine noodles
75 g (3 oz) butter
1 small onion, peeled and finely chopped
450 g (1 lb) small button mushrooms, cleaned
salt
freshly ground black pepper
2 tablespoons plain flour
350 ml (12 fl oz) double cream
120 ml (4 fl oz) dry white wine
2 eggs, beaten
50 ml (2 fl oz) milk
50 g (2 oz) freshly grated Parmesan cheese
1 tablespoon finely chopped fresh chives, to garnish

PREPARATION TIME: 15 minutes
COOKING TIME: 55 minutes
OVEN: 200°C, 400°F, Gas Mark 6

This is quite a rich dish, but good for quick entertaining. If you like, 250 g (8 oz) of cubed, cooked chicken can be added in Step 5.

1 Bring the water to the boil in a large saucepan over a high heat. Add the noodles and cook until almost tender. Drain well in a colander under warm water. Shake the colander to remove excess water. Place the noodles in a large bowl. Add 2 tablespoons of the butter. Toss the noodles well to coat. Set aside.

2 Melt the remaining butter in a large saucepan over a moderate heat. Add the onion and cook for 5 minutes, stirring frequently. Add the mushrooms, salt and pepper. Cook for 5 minutes, stirring occasionally.

3 Sprinkle the flour on the vegetable mixture. Cook for 2–3 minutes, stirring constantly. Using a whisk, gradually stir in the cream and wine. Cook for 2–3 minutes, stirring frequently. Remove the saucepan from the heat.

4 Combine the eggs and milk in a small bowl until well blended. Using a whisk, slowly stir into the creamed mushroom mixture.

5 Place the noodles in a large casserole. Pour the creamed mushroom mixture over the noodles and stir to combine. Sprinkle with the cheese and place in a preheated oven. Cook for 20 minutes.

6 Garnish with the chives, and serve accompanied by a green salad with plenty of tomatoes and French bread.

PAPRIKASH MEATBALLS

SERVES 6
450 g (1 lb) minced beef
1 egg, well beaten
50 g (2 oz) dried breadcrumbs
50 ml (2 fl oz) milk
1 tablespoon Hungarian paprika
1 tablespoon finely chopped fresh parsley
salt
freshly ground black pepper
2 tablespoons vegetable oil
1 medium onion, peeled and finely chopped
100 g (4 oz) button mushrooms, cleaned and sliced
1 teaspoon Hungarian paprika
350 ml (12 fl oz) beef stock
250 ml (8 fl oz) soured cream
1 tablespoon plain flour
6 sprigs fresh chervil, to garnish

PREPARATION TIME: 20 minutes
COOKING TIME: 55 minutes
OVEN: 180°C, 350°F, Gas Mark 4

1 For the meatballs, thoroughly combine the beef, egg, breadcrumbs, milk, tablespoon of paprika, parsley, salt and pepper in a large bowl. Shape the mixture into 24 × 4 cm (1½ inch) balls.

2 Heat the oil in a flameproof casserole. Add the meatballs and brown for 10 minutes, turning frequently. Using tongs, remove the meatballs from the casserole and set aside. Drain off all but 1 tablespoon of the fat in the casserole.

3 Add the onion, mushrooms and teaspoon of paprika to the casserole. Cook over a moderate heat for 5 minutes, stirring frequently. Return the meatballs to the casserole. Blend in the stock and cover. Place the casserole in a preheated oven and cook for 30 minutes.

4 Combine the soured cream and flour in a medium bowl until smooth. Place the casserole over a moderate heat on top of the stove. Using a whisk, stir the soured cream mixture into the casserole. Cook, stirring constantly, for 5 minutes until smooth and thickened. Taste the casserole and adjust the seasoning, if necessary.

5 To serve, garnish the casserole with the sprigs of fresh chervil.

SAUSAGES AND WHITE WINE CASSEROLE

350 ml (12 fl oz) dry white wine
250 ml (8 fl oz) beef stock
8 small onions, peeled
2 medium carrots, peeled and diced
1 tablespoon Dijon mustard
salt
freshly ground black pepper
1 tablespoon vegetable oil
750 g (1½ lb) pork sausages
1 tablespoon finely chopped parsley, to garnish

PREPARATION TIME: 15 minutes
COOKING TIME: 1 hour
OVEN: 180°C, 350°F, Gas Mark 4

1 Combine the wine, stock, onions, carrots, mustard, salt and pepper in a medium casserole. Cover and place in a preheated oven. Cook for 30 minutes.

2 Meanwhile, heat the oil in a large frying pan over a medium-low heat. Add the sausages and cook, turning frequently, for 5–7 minutes, until brown.

3 Stir the sausages into the casserole. Return the casserole to the oven. Cook, uncovered, for 30 minutes until the sausages are cooked through and the vegetables are tender.

4 Sprinkle the casserole with the parsley. Serve with creamed potatoes and a large green salad.

Clockwise from top left: Mushroom and Noodle Casserole; Paprikash Meatballs; Sausages and White Wine Casserole

GINGERED CITRUS CHICKEN

*4 × 150 g (5 oz) boneless chicken breasts, skin
removed*
½ teaspoon Hungarian paprika
salt
freshly ground black pepper
25 g (1 oz) butter
175 ml (6 fl oz) orange juice
50 ml (2 fl oz) lemon juice
grated rind of 1 lemon
1 teaspoon finely chopped peeled fresh ginger
2 teaspoons cornflour
2 tablespoons chicken stock

TO GARNISH:
2 tablespoons toasted slivered almonds
4 lemon twists
4 sprigs parsley

PREPARATION TIME: 15–20 minutes
COOKING TIME: 45–50 minutes
OVEN: 180°C, 350°F, Gas Mark 4

Gingered Citrus
Chicken

1 Sprinkle the chicken breasts with the paprika, salt and pepper. Set aside.

2 Melt the butter in a flameproof casserole over a moderate heat. Add the chicken and brown for 5–10 minutes, turning frequently. Drain off the excess fat.

3 Blend in the orange and lemon juices, the lemon rind and ginger. Cover and transfer to a preheated oven. Cook for 25–30 minutes, until the chicken is cooked through.

4 Remove the chicken from the casserole and place on a heated serving platter. Keep warm.

5 Pour the juice mixture into a small saucepan over a medium-high heat. Combine the cornflour and stock in a small cup until smooth. Using a whisk, stir into the juice mixture. Cook, stirring constantly, until the mixture comes to the boil. Cook for 1 minute, stirring constantly.

6 To serve, coat the chicken pieces with the citrus sauce. Sprinkle with the almonds, and garnish with the lemon twists and parsley sprigs.

CHICKEN, TOMATO AND OLIVE CASSEROLE
(Pollo à la Chilindron)

3 tablespoons olive or vegetable oil
8 chicken thighs, about 150 g (5 oz) each
2 large onions, peeled and chopped
1 large garlic clove, peeled and finely chopped
3 small red peppers, cored, seeded and cut into strips
6 medium tomatoes, peeled, seeded and chopped
100 g (4 oz) ham, diced
75 g (3 oz) stoned green olives
salt
freshly ground black pepper
300 ml (½ pint) chicken stock
1 bunch watercress, to garnish (optional)

PREPARATION TIME: 30 minutes
COOKING TIME: 1¼ hours

1 Heat the oil in a large flameproof casserole over a medium-high heat. Add the chicken thighs and brown on all sides for 10 minutes, turning frequently. Using a pair of tongs, transfer the chicken to paper towels and drain. Set aside.

2 Pour off all but 1 tablespoon of the fat in the casserole. Add the onions and garlic, then cook over a moderate heat for 5 minutes, stirring frequently. Add the peppers and tomatoes. Cook for 10 minutes, stirring occasionally. Blend in the ham and olives. Place the chicken pieces on top of the vegetable mixture. Sprinkle with the salt and pepper, then pour in the stock. Cover and simmer for 40 minutes until the chicken is cooked through.

3 Transfer the chicken to a heated serving platter and keep warm. Cook the sauce in the casserole, uncovered, for 5 minutes to thicken.

4 To serve, pour the sauce over the chicken. Garnish with the watercress, if liked, and serve with steamed rice or crusty bread.

Chicken, Tomato and Olive Casserole

BOEUF RAGOÛT

40 g (1½ oz) butter
1 large onion, peeled and thinly sliced
1 garlic clove, peeled and finely chopped
275 g (10 oz) cooked beef, cubed
2 medium carrots, peeled and diced
1 medium potato, peeled and diced
350 ml (12 fl oz) beef stock
175 ml (6 fl oz) leftover gravy
2 teaspoons red wine vinegar
salt
freshly ground black pepper

TO FINISH:
2 tablespoons cornflour
50 ml (2 fl oz) red wine or beef stock
finely chopped fresh parsley, to garnish (optional)

PREPARATION TIME: 20 minutes
COOKING TIME: 40 minutes

1 Melt the butter in a flameproof casserole over a moderate heat. Add the onion and cook for 8 minutes, stirring frequently. Add the garlic and cook for 2 minutes, stirring frequently.

2 Add the beef, carrots, potato, stock, gravy, vinegar, salt and pepper to the casserole. Bring to the boil, then cover and reduce the heat to moderate. Simmer gently for 25 minutes, stirring the casserole occasionally.

3 Combine the cornflour and wine in a cup until smooth. Using a whisk, stir into the ragoût. Bring the mixture to the boil, stirring constantly, until the sauce is smooth and thick.

4 To serve, sprinkle the ragoût with the parsley, if liked.

Left to right: Boeuf Ragoût; Red Flannel Hash; Spicy Beef and Bean Casserole

RED FLANNEL HASH

4 medium potatoes, peeled and diced
1.2 litres (2 pints) water
40 g (1½ oz) butter
2 medium onions, peeled and chopped
4 tablespoons plain flour
900 ml (1½ pints) beef stock
85 ml (3 fl oz) double cream
750 g (1½ lb) corned beef, trimmed and diced
12 small cooked beets, trimmed and diced
salt
freshly ground black pepper
sprigs of watercress, to garnish

PREPARATION TIME: 25 minutes
COOKING TIME: 45 minutes

Hash is a time-honoured dish, starting in France as 'haché' or 'hachis' which means something cut up. Usually it consisted of a mixture of cooked meat, vegetables and gravy, seasoned and then served. 'Haché' crossed the Channel as 'hash', Samuel Pepys writing in his diary of having 'a hash of rabbits'. Continuing its journey westward, hash arrived in North America. Here is a popular hash recipe, using corned beef, potatoes and beets. The beets colour the dish red – hence its name.

1 Place the potatoes and water in a medium saucepan over a high heat. Bring to the boil, then reduce the heat to moderate. Cook for 15 minutes, until the potatoes are just tender. Drain the potatoes in a colander and set aside.

2 Meanwhile, melt the butter in a flameproof casserole over a moderate heat. Add the onions and cook for 10 minutes, stirring frequently. Sprinkle the flour on the onions and stir well to combine. Cook for 2–3 minutes, stirring constantly. Using a whisk, gradually stir in the stock and cream. Cook for 5 minutes, stirring constantly, until smooth and thick.

3 Blend the potatoes, corned beef, beets, salt and pepper into the casserole. Cover and cook over a medium-low heat for 20 minutes.

4 Remove the casserole from the heat and uncover. Garnish with the watercress.

SPICY BEEF AND BEAN CASSEROLE

SERVES 6

450 g (1 lb) minced beef
1 medium onion, peeled and chopped
1 green pepper, cored, seeded and chopped
1 garlic clove, peeled and finely chopped
1 × 400 g (14 oz) can tomatoes
1 × 400 g (14 oz) can kidney beans, drained
1 × 400 g (14 oz) can butter beans, undrained
250 ml (8 fl oz) tomato sauce
1 × 150 g (5 oz) can tomato purée
2 teaspoons chilli powder
salt
freshly ground black pepper
100 g (4 oz) Cheddar cheese, grated, to garnish

PREPARATION TIME: 15 minutes
COOKING TIME: 40 minutes

Tortillas, guacamole, salad garnishes such as shredded lettuce, tomatoes and spring onions, plus more hot sauce on the table would make this casserole a complete meal.

1 Place the mince, onion, green pepper and garlic in a flameproof casserole. Cook over a moderate heat, stirring frequently to break up the meat, for 10 minutes or until the meat is no longer pink. Drain off the excess fat. Blend in the remaining ingredients. Cover and simmer gently for 30 minutes, stirring occasionally.

2 To serve, sprinkle with the cheese.

PAPRIKA PORK CHOPS

25 g (1 oz) plain flour
2 tablespoons Hungarian paprika
¼ teaspoon cayenne pepper
salt
freshly ground black pepper
4 × 175 g (6 oz) loin pork chops
1 tablespoon vegetable oil
4 medium potatoes, peeled and thinly sliced
1 large onion, peeled and thinly sliced
300 ml (½ pint) beef stock
300 ml (½ pint) soured cream
2 tablespoons plain flour

TO GARNISH:
1 bunch watercress
1 teaspoon caraway seeds (optional)

PREPARATION TIME: 25 minutes
COOKING TIME: 1 hour
OVEN: 190°C, 375°F, Gas Mark 5

1 Combine the flour, paprika, cayenne pepper, salt and pepper on a large plate. Coat the pork chops in this mixture. Set aside.

2 Heat the oil in a large flameproof casserole over a moderate heat. Add the pork chops and brown for 10 minutes, turning frequently. Remove the chops with tongs and set aside.

3 Lay the potato and onion slices on the bottom of the casserole. Place the pork chops on top of the slices. Pour the stock into the casserole. Cover and place in a preheated oven. Cook for 45 minutes.

4 Combine the soured cream and flour until smooth. Set aside.

5 Remove the pork chops and vegetables from the casserole. Arrange on a heated serving platter and keep warm. Place the casserole over a medium-low heat. Using a whisk, stir in the soured cream mixture. Cook until just heated through. Remove the sauce from the heat and pour over the chops. Garnish with the watercress and caraway seeds, if using, then serve immediately.

From the top: Paprika Pork Chops; Orange and Liver Casserole; Cider Pork Chops

ORANGE AND LIVER CASSEROLE

25 g (1 oz) plain flour
salt
freshly ground black pepper
1 kg (2 lb) lamb's liver, thinly sliced
40 g (1½ oz) butter
2 tablespoons vegetable oil
1 medium onion, peeled and thinly sliced
1 garlic clove, peeled and finely chopped
2 oranges, thinly sliced and seeds removed
250 ml (8 fl oz) dry red wine
250 ml (8 fl oz) orange juice
2 tablespoons orange marmalade
2 tablespoons thyme leaves or 1 teaspoon dried thyme
2 tablespoons double cream
1 tablespoon finely chopped fresh parsley, to garnish

PREPARATION TIME: 20 minutes
COOKING TIME: 45 minutes
OVEN: 140°C, 275°F, Gas Mark 1

The liver for this recipe should be very thinly sliced. The fresh liver sold in some butchers' shops is not sliced thinly enough, so you may prefer to buy frozen liver. When it has partially thawed, carefully slice it with a sharp knife.

1 Combine the flour, salt and pepper on a large plate. Coat the liver with the flour, shaking off the excess. Set aside.

2 Heat the butter and oil in a large frying pan over a moderate heat. Add the onion and garlic, then cook for 5 minutes, stirring occasionally. Transfer the onion and garlic with a slotted spoon to a large casserole and set aside.

3 Add the liver slices to the frying pan. Cook on one side for 2–3 minutes until brown, then turn the slices over. Cook on the other side for 2 minutes. Transfer the liver with a slotted spoon to the casserole and set aside.

4 Add the orange slices to the frying pan. Cook for 1–2 minutes, turning frequently. Transfer the orange slices with a slotted spoon over the liver in the casserole and set aside.

5 Add the wine, orange juice, marmalade, thyme, salt and pepper to the frying pan. Bring to the boil, stirring constantly, then pour over the ingredients in the casserole.

6 Cover and place the casserole in a preheated oven. Cook for 30 minutes.

7 Remove the casserole from the oven and stir in the cream. Garnish with the parsley.

CIDER PORK CHOPS

4 × 175 g (6 oz) loin pork chops
salt
freshly ground black pepper
2 tablespoons vegetable oil
15 g (½ oz) butter
1 medium onion, peeled and thinly sliced
1 cooking apple, cored and chopped
225 g (8 oz) button mushrooms, cleaned and sliced
1 large garlic clove, peeled and finely chopped
1 tablespoon fresh thyme leaves or ½ teaspoon dried thyme
1 tablespoon finely chopped fresh rosemary or ½ teaspoon dried rosemary
350 ml (12 fl oz) dry cider
150 ml (¼ pint) double cream

PREPARATION TIME: 15 minutes
COOKING TIME: 1¼ hours

1 Season the pork chops with the salt and pepper. Set aside.

2 Heat the oil and butter in a flameproof casserole over a moderate heat. Add the pork chops and brown on both sides for 10 minutes, turning frequently. Using a pair of tongs, remove the chops from the casserole and set aside.

3 Add the onion, apple, mushrooms and garlic to the casserole. Cook over a moderate heat for 5 minutes, stirring frequently. Push the mixture to one side of the casserole. Return the chops to the casserole. Add the thyme and rosemary. Spoon the onion mixture over the chops, then add the cider. Reduce the heat to low and cover. Simmer for 45 minutes.

4 Remove the cover and transfer the chops to a heated serving platter. Keep warm. Raise the heat under the casserole to moderate. Stir in the cream. Bring the sauce to a simmer and let it reduce slightly, stirring frequently. Taste the sauce and adjust the seasoning, if necessary.

5 To serve, pour the sauce over the chops. Serve with creamed potatoes and red cabbage.

CALF'S LIVER WITH MUSHROOMS AND OLIVES

SERVES 6

15 g (½ oz) butter, for greasing
1 kg (2 lb) thinly sliced calf's liver
100 g (4 oz) button mushrooms, cleaned and sliced
100 g (4 oz) stoned ripe olives
1 medium onion, peeled and chopped
1 green pepper, cored, seeded and chopped
1 garlic clove, peeled and finely chopped
2 × 400 g (14 oz) cans tomatoes
120 ml (4 fl oz) tomato ketchup
50 ml (2 fl oz) beef stock
2 tablespoons finely chopped fresh oregano or 1 teaspoon dried oregano
1 tablespoon finely chopped fresh parsley
salt
freshly ground black pepper
2 tablespoons olive oil
1 tablespoon plain flour

PREPARATION TIME: 15 minutes
COOKING TIME: 30–40 minutes
OVEN: 180°C, 350°F, Gas Mark 4

This recipe is very simple to assemble. You don't even have to brown the liver before placing it in the casserole. What an appropriate way of enjoying, as the Italians say, the 'dolce vita'!

1 Grease a large casserole with the butter. Place the liver slices in the casserole. Set aside.

2 Combine the mushrooms, olives, onion, pepper, garlic, tomatoes, ketchup, stock, oregano, parsley, salt and pepper in a large bowl until well blended. Combine the oil and flour in a cup until smooth. Stir into the sauce mixture. Pour the sauce over the liver slices and place the casserole in a preheated oven. Cook for 30–40 minutes until tender.

3 Serve with rice and a vegetable of your choice.

LAMBS' KIDNEYS IN RED WINE

8 lambs' kidneys
900 ml (1½ pints) water
salt
25 g (1 oz) butter
2 tablespoons plain flour
300 ml (½ pint) dry red wine
300 ml (½ pint) beef or lamb stock
3 tablespoons finely chopped fresh parsley
1 garlic clove, peeled and finely chopped
freshly ground black pepper

PREPARATION TIME: 10 minutes, plus soaking time
COOKING TIME: 40 minutes
OVEN: 180°C, 350°F, Gas Mark 4

If your budget can stretch to veal kidneys, try substituting them for the lambs' kidneys. Presoaking would not be necessary, but the white core should be removed. Veal kidneys should be cut into large slices.

1 Place the kidneys in a medium bowl. Cover with the water, then add the salt. Soak for 30 minutes.

2 Drain the kidneys. Remove the skin and cut the kidneys in half. Remove the white core, then set the kidneys aside.

3 Melt the butter over a medium-high heat in a flameproof casserole. Add the kidneys and cook for 2–3 minutes, stirring frequently. Sprinkle the flour on the kidneys and stir well to combine. Gradually stir in the wine and stock. Bring the sauce to the boil stirring continuously, then add the parsley, garlic, salt and pepper. Cover the casserole and place in a preheated oven. Cook for 30 minutes.

4 Serve with hot, buttered toast.

Clockwise from top left: Calf's Liver with Mushrooms and Olives; Lamb's Kidneys in Red Wine; Frankfurter and Vegetable Casserole

FRANKFURTER AND VEGETABLE CASSEROLE

2 tablespoons vegetable oil
1 large onion, peeled and thinly sliced
1 green pepper, cored, seeded and cubed
1 red pepper, cored, seeded and cubed
1 green chilli pepper, seeded and finely chopped
1 garlic clove, peeled and finely chopped
2 × 400 g (14 oz) cans tomatoes
1 tablespoon demerara sugar
salt
freshly ground black pepper
8 frankfurters

PREPARATION TIME: 15 minutes
COOKING TIME: 45 minutes

1 Heat the oil in a flameproof casserole over a moderate heat. Add the onion and cook for 5 minutes, stirring frequently. Add the peppers and garlic, then cook for 5 minutes, stirring frequently. Blend in the tomatoes. Add the sugar, salt and pepper. Place the frankfurters in the casserole.

2 Cover the casserole and cook for 30 minutes, stirring occasionally.

PIQUANT TUNA AND EGG

40 g (1½ oz) butter
40 g (1½ oz) plain flour
350 ml (12 fl oz) milk
salt
freshly ground white pepper
2 × 200 g (7 oz) cans tuna, drained and broken into chunks
2 hard-boiled eggs, shelled and chopped
1 red pepper, cored, seeded and chopped
3 tablespoons finely chopped fresh parsley
2 teaspoons lemon juice
2 teaspoons prepared mustard
½ teaspoon drained prepared horseradish

PREPARATION TIME: 10 minutes
COOKING TIME: 25–30 minutes
OVEN: 180°C, 350°F, Gas Mark 4

1 Melt the butter in a medium saucepan over a moderate heat. Blend in the flour. Cook, stirring frequently, for 2–3 minutes. Using a whisk, gradually stir in the milk. Cook, stirring constantly, until smooth and thickened. Season with the salt and pepper, then remove from the heat. Place the sauce in a large heatproof bowl.

2 Add the remaining ingredients to the sauce, mixing well. Lightly mix in the tuna, egg and red pepper. Place the mixture in a medium casserole. [A] Cover and cook in a preheated oven for 15–20 minutes, until hot and bubbly.

3 Serve with a rice pilaff and buttered spinach.

[A] Can be prepared several hours in advance, covered and kept chilled. Allow to stand at room temperature for 1 hour before proceeding with the recipe.

SMOKED HADDOCK AND POTATO CASSEROLE

FOR THE POTATOES:
4 medium potatoes, peeled and cut into chunks
1.2 litres (2 pints) water
4 tablespoons Greek-style plain, unsweetened yogurt
15 g (½ oz) butter
¼ teaspoon freshly grated nutmeg
salt
freshly ground white pepper

FOR THE HADDOCK:
750 g (1½ lb) smoked haddock
475 ml (16 fl oz) milk
1 bay leaf
50 g (2 oz) butter
50 g (2 oz) plain flour
50 g (2 oz) Cheddar cheese, grated

PREPARATION TIME: 20 minutes
COOKING TIME: 1 hour
OVEN: 180°C, 350°F, Gas Mark 4

1 Combine the potatoes and water in a large saucepan. Bring to the boil over a high heat, then lower the heat to a simmer. Cook for 15–20 minutes, until tender. Drain well in a colander, then return the potatoes to the saucepan. Add the yogurt, butter, nutmeg, salt and pepper. Mash until smooth. Pipe or spoon the potatoes around the sides of a medium casserole dish. Set aside.

2 Meanwhile, combine the haddock, milk and bay leaf in a large saucepan. Cover and bring to a simmer over a moderate heat. Cook for 5 minutes. Strain off the cooking liquid and reserve. Discard the bay leaf. Remove the skin from the haddock, then flake the fish. Set aside.

3 Melt the butter in the same saucepan over a moderate heat. Add the flour and cook for 2–3 minutes, stirring constantly. Using a whisk, gradually stir in the cooking liquid. Cook until smooth and thickened. Return the flaked haddock to the sauce, then remove from the heat. Pour the mixture into the casserole dish. Sprinkle with the cheese, then place, uncovered, in a preheated oven. Cook for 30 minutes, until hot and bubbly.

BELGIUM FISH CASSEROLE

175 ml (6 fl oz) fish stock
120 ml (4 fl oz) dry white wine
2 tablespoons lemon juice
1 tablespoon fresh thyme leaves or ½ teaspoon dried thyme
1 bay leaf, crushed
salt
freshly ground black pepper
25 g (1 oz) butter
2 medium carrots, peeled and julienned
2 leeks, white part only, julienned
1 celery stick, julienned
450 g (1 lb) boneless, skinned cod fillets

TO GARNISH:
1 tablespoon finely chopped fresh chives
4 lemon wedges

PREPARATION TIME: 20 minutes
COOKING TIME: 20–25 minutes
OVEN: 180°C, 350°F, Gas Mark 4

1 Combine the stock, wine, lemon juice, thyme, bay leaf, salt and pepper in a medium bowl. Set aside.

2 Melt the butter in a large flameproof casserole over a moderate heat. Add the carrots, leeks and celery. Cook for 5 minutes, stirring frequently. Place the fish on top of the vegetables in the casserole. Pour the stock mixture over the fish. Cover and place in a preheated oven. Cook for 10–15 minutes or until the fish flakes easily when tested with a fork.

3 Remove the fish to a heated serving platter and keep warm. Boil the vegetable mixture, uncovered, over a moderate heat for 5 minutes or until the liquid is reduced by half.

4 To serve, spoon the vegetable mixture over the fish fillets. Sprinkle with the chives and garnish with the lemon wedges. Serve immediately.

Clockwise from left: Piquant Tuna and Egg;
Smoked Haddock and Potato Casserole; Belgium
Fish Casserole

TUNA CAROUSEL

15 g (½ oz) butter, for greasing
1 × 200 g (7 oz) can tuna, drained and flaked
225 g (8 oz) frozen peas, thawed
100 g (4 oz) button mushrooms, cleaned and sliced
1 garlic clove, peeled and finely chopped
¼ teaspoon dillweed
¼ teaspoon celery seed
salt
freshly ground black pepper

FOR THE SAUCE:
50 g (2 oz) butter
50 g (2 oz) plain flour
475 ml (16 fl oz) milk
2 tablespoons dry sherry
salt
freshly ground white pepper

TO FINISH:
350 g (12 oz) cooked noodles
25 g (1 oz) fresh white breadcrumbs

PREPARATION TIME: 15 minutes
COOKING TIME: 40 minutes
OVEN: 180°C, 350°F, Gas Mark 4

1 Grease a medium casserole with the butter. Combine the tuna, peas, mushrooms, garlic, dillweed, celery seed, salt and pepper in a bowl. Transfer to the casserole and set aside.

2 For the sauce, melt the butter in a medium saucepan over a moderate heat. Add the flour and cook for 2–3 minutes, stirring constantly. Using a whisk, gradually stir in the milk. Cook, stirring constantly, until smooth and thickened. Blend in the sherry, salt and pepper. Remove from the heat.

3 Stir half of the sauce into the tuna mixture. Spread the noodles over the tuna. Pour the remaining sauce into the noodles. Sprinkle the breadcrumbs over the noodles. [A] Transfer the uncovered casserole to a preheated oven and cook for 30 minutes until hot and bubbly.

[A] Can be prepared earlier in the day, covered and kept chilled.

From the top: Tuna Carousel; Creamy Finnan Haddie Casserole; Salmon Corn Casserole

CREAMY FINNAN HADDIE CASSEROLE

450 g (1 lb) boneless finnan haddie
750 ml (1¼ pints) boiling water
50 g (2 oz) butter
50 g (2 oz) plain flour
350 ml (12 fl oz) single cream
¼ teaspoon paprika
salt (optional)
freshly ground white pepper
50 g (2 oz) Cheddar cheese, grated
15 g (½ oz) butter, for greasing
25 g (1 oz) soft white breadcrumbs
25 g (1 oz) Cheddar cheese, grated

TO GARNISH:
4 lemon wedges (optional)
sprig parsley

PREPARATION TIME: 15 minutes
COOKING TIME: 35 minutes
OVEN: 190°C, 375°F, Gas Mark 5

1 Place the fish in a medium saucepan. Cover with the boiling water. Simmer over a low heat for 10 minutes, until the fish flakes easily. Drain, then flake the fish into a medium bowl. Set aside.

2 Melt the butter in a small saucepan over a moderate heat. Blend in the flour and cook for 2–3 minutes, stirring constantly. Using a whisk, gradually stir in the cream. Bring the sauce to a simmer and cook, stirring constantly, until thick and smooth. Remove from the heat, then add the paprika, salt, if using, and pepper.

3 Blend the sauce with the fish. Add the cheese and stir well.

4 Grease a medium casserole with the butter. Pour the fish mixture into the casserole. Top with the breadcrumbs and cheese. [A] Place in a preheated oven and cook for 20–25 minutes, until the top is brown.

5 Garnish with the lemon wedges, if liked, and parsley sprig. Serve immediately with toast and a cucumber salad.

[A] Can be prepared several hours in advance, covered and chilled. Allow to stand at room temperature for 1 hour before proceeding with the recipe.

SALMON CORN CASSEROLE

SERVES 6
25 g (1 oz) butter
3 × 285 g (10½ oz) cans cream-style corn
1 × 425 g (15 oz) can salmon
3 eggs, beaten
25 g (1 oz) cheese cracker crumbs, reserve 1 tablespoon for topping
salt
freshly ground pepper

TO GARNISH:
6 lemon wedges
sprig parsley

PREPARATION TIME: 10 minutes
COOKING TIME: 1 hour
OVEN: 180°C, 350°F, Gas Mark 4

1 Grease a medium casserole with 1 tablespoon of the butter. Set aside.

2 Combine the corn, salmon, eggs, cracker crumbs, salt and pepper in a large bowl. Transfer the mixture to the casserole. Top the casserole with the reserved cracker crumbs and dot with the remaining butter. Transfer the uncovered casserole to a preheated oven and cook for 1 hour.

3 Garnish the casserole with the lemon wedges and parsley. Serve with a green salad for a light and quick meal.

ORANGE-PINEAPPLE CHICKEN

1 × 1¾ kg (4 lb) chicken, quartered
salt
freshly ground white pepper
2 tablespoons vegetable oil
25 g (1 oz) butter
175 ml (6 fl oz) orange juice
2 × 225 g (8 oz) cans pineapple chunks, the juice
reserved (recipe needs 250 ml/8 fl oz)
extra pineapple juice, if necessary
3 lemon slices
50 g (2 oz) skinned almonds, toasted
sprigs flat leaf parsley, to garnish

PREPARATION TIME: 10 minutes
COOKING TIME: 1 hour
OVEN: 180°C, 350°F, Gas Mark 4

1 Season the chicken with the salt and pepper. Set aside.

2 Heat the oil and butter in a flameproof casserole over a medium-high heat. Add the chicken, skin side down, and brown for 10 minutes, turning frequently. Transfer the chicken with tongs to a plate. Drain off the excess fat from the casserole. Add the orange juice and, scraping the casserole bottom to incorporate all the bits, bring to a simmer. Return the chicken to the casserole, coating with the orange juice mixture. Cover the casserole and place in a preheated oven. Cook for 25 minutes.

3 Add the pineapple, 120 ml (4 fl oz) of the pineapple juice and lemon slices. Cover and return to the oven. Cook for 15 minutes.

4 Add the remaining pineapple juice (120 ml/4 fl oz) and almonds to the casserole. Return to the oven and cook, uncovered, for 5 minutes.

5 Arrange the chicken on a heated serving platter. Pour the sauce over the pieces, then garnish with the parsley. Serve with steamed rice and stir-fried green vegetables.

Orange-Pineapple Chicken

CHICKEN NOODLE CASSEROLE WITH ALMONDS

SERVES 4-6

FOR THE NOODLES:
2.75 litres (5 pints) water
1 tablespoon olive oil
salt
450 g (1 lb) green fettucine noodles

FOR THE CASSEROLE:
50 g (2 oz) butter
1 shallot, peeled and finely chopped
4 tablespoons plain flour
250 ml (8 fl oz) double cream
475 ml (16 fl oz) chicken stock
1 tablespoon chopped fresh parsley
salt
freshly ground white pepper
15 g (½ oz) butter, for greasing
450 g (1 lb) cooked chicken meat, cubed
50 g (2 oz) slivered almonds, toasted

PREPARATION TIME: 20 minutes
COOKING TIME: 40 minutes
OVEN: 180°C, 350°F, Gas Mark 4

1 For the noodles, bring the water, oil and salt to the boil in a large saucepan over a high heat. Add the noodles. Cook for 5–7 minutes, until just tender. Drain and rinse in a colander.

2 Meanwhile, melt the butter in a medium saucepan over a moderate heat. Add the shallot and cook for 2–3 minutes, stirring frequently. Blend in the flour. Cook for 2–3 minutes, stirring constantly. Using a whisk, gradually stir in the cream and stock. Cook, stirring constantly, until smooth and thick. Remove the sauce from the heat, stir in the parsley and season with the salt and pepper. Set aside.

3 Grease a medium casserole with the butter. Place the noodles evenly on the bottom of the casserole. Top with the chicken. Sprinkle half the almonds evenly over the chicken. Pour the sauce over the mixture. [A] Cook the covered casserole in a preheated oven for 20 minutes.

4 Remove the casserole from the oven. Garnish with the remaining almonds.

[A] Can be prepared several hours in advance, covered and chilled. Stand at room temperature for 1 hour before proceeding.

Chicken Noodle
Casserole with Almonds

SAUSAGE AND APPLE CASSEROLE

25 g (1 oz) butter
750 g (1½ lb) pork sausages
1 medium onion, peeled and chopped
2 tablespoons demerara sugar
½ teaspoon allspice
salt
freshly ground black pepper
2 cooking apples, cored and sliced

TO FINISH:
25 g (1 oz) butter
25 g (1 oz) plain flour
600 ml (1 pint) beef stock
1 tablespoon finely chopped fresh parsley, to garnish

PREPARATION TIME: 15 minutes
COOKING TIME: 1 hour
OVEN: 190°C, 375°F, Gas Mark 5

1 Melt all but 1 tablespoon of the butter in a large frying pan over a moderate heat. Add the sausages and brown for 5 minutes, turning frequently. Remove the sausages with a pair of tongs to drain on paper towels. Set aside.

2 Add the onion to the frying pan. Cook for 5 minutes over a moderate heat, stirring frequently. Remove the onion with a slotted spoon and set aside. Reserve the fat in the pan.

3 Grease a large casserole with the remaining butter. Arrange the sausages in the casserole. Sprinkle with a third of the sugar, allspice, salt and pepper. Top with the onion. Sprinkle with a third of the sugar, allspice, salt and pepper. Arrange the apple slices over the onion. Season with the remaining sugar, allspice, salt and pepper. Set aside.

4 Melt the butter in a small saucepan over a moderate heat. Add the flour and cook for 2–3 minutes, stirring constantly. Using a whisk, gradually stir in the stock. Bring the mixture to the boil, stirring constantly, and cook until smooth and thickened. Pour the sauce over the casserole. [A] Cover and place in a preheated oven. Cook for 45 minutes.

5 To serve, sprinkle the casserole with the parsley. Creamed potatoes and a stir-fry of carrot and courgette sticks are excellent accompaniments.

[A] Can be prepared several hours in advance, then covered and kept chilled. Allow to stand at room temperature for 1 hour before proceeding with the recipe.

CHICORY AND HAM ROLLS GOURMET

1 tablespoon butter, for greasing
2.25 litres (4 pints) water
2 tablespoons lemon juice
12 heads chicory, bases trimmed
12 slices thin ham
¼ teaspoon freshly ground nutmeg
salt
freshly ground white pepper
2 hard-boiled eggs, shelled and sliced

FOR THE SAUCE:
50 g (2 oz) butter
50 g (2 oz) plain flour
475 ml (16 fl oz) milk
100 g (4 oz) Edam cheese, grated

FOR THE TOPPING:
25 g (1 oz) buttered breadcrumbs
25 g (1 oz) Edam cheese, grated

PREPARATION TIME: 15 minutes
COOKING TIME: 55 minutes
OVEN: 190°C, 375°F, Gas Mark 5

1 Grease a medium casserole with the butter, then set aside.

2 Bring the water and lemon juice to a simmer in a large saucepan. Add the chicory and lower the heat. Cook for 10 minutes until the heads are tender but still firm. Drain the chicory.

3 Wrap each head of chicory in a slice of ham and arrange the rolls in the casserole. Sprinkle with the nutmeg, salt and pepper. Top with the egg slices. Cover and set aside.

4 For the sauce, melt the butter in a medium saucepan over a moderate heat. Blend in the flour. Cook for 2–3 minutes, stirring constantly. Using a whisk, gradually stir in the milk. Cook, stirring constantly, until smooth and thick. Add the cheese and cook until just melted. Remove the saucepan from the heat, then add salt and pepper to taste. Pour the sauce over the casserole.

5 For the topping, sprinkle the casserole with the buttered breadcrumbs and cheese. [A] Cook in a preheated oven for 35 minutes.

6 Serve with a tomato salad.

[A] Can be prepared several hours in advance, covered and kept chilled. Allow to stand at room temperature for 1 hour before proceeding with the recipe.

COURGETTE AND BACON CASSEROLE

SERVES 6
2.25 litres (4 pints) water
1 kg (2 lb) small courgettes, sliced
4 eggs, beaten
450 ml (¾ pint) milk
250 g (8 oz) Cheddar cheese, grated
¼ teaspoon paprika
salt
freshly ground black pepper
1 tablespoon butter, for greasing
100 g (4 oz) streaky bacon, grilled until crisp and
crumbled

PREPARATION TIME: 30 minutes
COOKING TIME: 1 hour
OVEN: 180°C, 350°F, Gas Mark 4

1 Bring the water to the boil in a large saucepan over a high heat. Add the courgettes and cook for 2 minutes. Drain the courgettes in a colander under cold running water. Shake the colander well to remove excess water.

2 Combine the eggs and milk in a large bowl. Stir in 150 g (5 oz) of the cheese. Add the paprika, salt and pepper.

3 Grease a medium casserole dish with the butter. Place half of the courgettes in the dish. Sprinkle the courgettes with the bacon. Top with the remaining courgettes. Pour the egg mixture into the casserole. Sprinkle with the remaining cheese. [A] Place in a preheated oven and cook for 35–40 minutes until set and the top is golden brown.

4 Serve with a mixed salad and hot bread.

[A] Can be prepared several hours in advance, then covered and kept chilled. Allow to stand at room temperature for 1 hour before proceeding with the recipe.

Clockwise from top left: Sausage and Apple Casserole; Courgette and Bacon Casserole; Chicory and Ham Rolls Gourmet

TURKEY RICE CASSEROLE

50 g (2 oz) butter
2 medium onions, peeled and chopped
225 g (8 oz) button mushrooms, cleaned and sliced
225 g (8 oz) cooked turkey, cubed
150 g (5 oz) stuffing, cubed or crumbled
100 g (4 oz) ham, diced
2 tablespoons finely chopped fresh parsley
½ tablespoon fresh thyme leaves or ½ teaspoon dried thyme
salt
freshly ground black pepper
200 g (7 oz) long-grain rice
1 tablespoon mild curry powder
475 ml (16 fl oz) hot turkey or chicken stock

PREPARATION TIME: 25 minutes
COOKING TIME: 1 hour
OVEN: 190°C, 375°F, Gas Mark 5

This is a good recipe for that perennial holiday problem – what to do with the left-over turkey and stuffing. This one is easy on the cook and has a mildly exotic flavour. Use homemade stuffing, not a packaged version.

1 Melt 40 g (1½ oz) of the butter in a large saucepan over a moderate heat. Add the onions and cook for 5 minutes, stirring frequently. Add the mushrooms and continue to cook for another 5 minutes, stirring frequently. Place the vegetable mixture in a medium casserole. Add the turkey, stuffing, ham, parsley, thyme, salt and pepper, then stir well to combine. Set aside.

2 In the saucepan used to cook the onions, melt the remaining butter over a moderate heat. Add the rice and curry powder. Brown, stirring frequently, for 5 minutes. Remove the pan from the heat and stir the mixture into the casserole. Pour in the hot stock and cover. Transfer to a preheated oven and cook for 40 minutes, until the rice is tender and the stock is absorbed.

3 Serve with chutney and a minted cucumber-yogurt salad.

Turkey Rice Casserole

CHICKEN LIVER CASSEROLE

100 g (4 oz) butter
450 g (1 lb) chicken livers
1 medium onion, peeled and finely chopped
100 g (4 oz) button mushrooms, cleaned and thinly sliced
15 g (½ oz) plain flour
450 ml (¾ pint) milk
2 tablespoons finely chopped fresh parsley
salt
freshly ground black pepper
2 red peppers, cored, seeded and cut into rings

PREPARATION TIME: 15 minutes
COOKING TIME: 45 minutes
OVEN: 180°C, 350°F, Gas Mark 4

1 Melt all but 15 g (½ oz) of the butter in a medium frying pan over a moderate heat. Add the livers and cook for 5 minutes, stirring frequently, until brown. Remove the livers from the pan with a slotted spoon and set aside.

2 Add the onion and mushrooms to the pan. Cook over a moderate heat for 5 minutes, stirring frequently. Blend in the flour. Cook for 2–3 minutes, stirring constantly. Using a whisk, gradually stir in the milk. Cook, stirring constantly, until the sauce is smooth and thick. Add the parsley, salt and pepper, then remove the sauce from the heat.

3 Grease a medium casserole with the remaining butter. Arrange the livers in the casserole. Top with the pepper rings. Pour the sauce over the casserole. [A] Cover and place in a preheated oven. Cook for 30 minutes until hot.

4 Serve the casserole with steamed rice and crisp stir-fried vegetables.

[A] Can be prepared 1 hour in advance and covered.

Chicken Liver Casserole

CLASSIC CASSEROLES

*The casseroles in this chapter bear famous names
– Coq au Vin, Boeuf à la Mode, Cassoulet,
Lancashire Hot Pot, Osso Bucco – for this is a
selection of some of the great casseroles from the
cuisines of many countries. The choice of recipes
covers the range of casserole techniques including
the initial marinating, often in wine, to help
achieve mouth-wateringly tender meat, as in
Boeuf Bourguignon; and the long, slow cooking
to bring out the casserole's subtle flavour as in
Boeuf en Daube, or Oxtail Casserole. The
sometimes surprising combination of ingredients
to provide an unforgettable taste features in such
classics as Chicken Marengo and the addition of
tasty toppings is demonstrated on Beef Cobbler
and Carbonnade de Boeuf.*

CHICKEN MARENGO

1 × 1.75 kg (4 lb) chicken
salt
freshly ground black pepper
50 g (2 oz) butter
2 tablespoons brandy
1 onion, peeled and sliced
1-2 garlic cloves, peeled and crushed
2 tablespoons flour
1 × 425 g (15 oz) can tomatoes, liquidized, puréed
or very finely chopped
150 ml (¼ pint) dry white wine
1 tablespoon tomato purée
100 g (4 oz) button mushrooms, trimmed and halved

TO GARNISH:
4 crayfish or 8 large whole prawns
25 g (1 oz) butter
2 hard-boiled eggs, shelled and quartered
few slices pickled walnut or 8 black olives

PREPARATION TIME: 20 minutes
COOKING TIME: about 50 minutes
OVEN: 180°C, 350°F, Gas Mark 4

1 Cut the chicken into 8 even-sized pieces and remove the skin. Sprinkle with salt and pepper.

2 Melt 25 g (1 oz) of the butter in a pan, add the chicken pieces and brown on all sides. Transfer to a casserole.

3 Warm the brandy, pour over the chicken and ignite carefully.

4 When the flames have died down, add the remaining butter to the pan and then add the onion and garlic. Fry gently until lightly coloured.

5 Add the flour to the onions and cook for 1 minute. Gradually add the tomatoes, wine and tomato purée and bring to the boil.

6 Add salt and pepper and the mushrooms and simmer for 2 minutes. Pour over the chicken and cover the casserole.

7 Cook in a preheated oven for 45–50 minutes or until tender.

8 For the garnish, lightly fry the crayfish or prawns in butter. Arrange the chicken pieces on a deep serving plate, spoon the sauce over and garnish with crayfish or prawns, quarters of hard-boiled egg and slices of pickled walnut or black olives.

COQ AU VIN

45 g (1¾ oz) butter
100 g (4 oz) thick unsmoked streaky bacon, rind
removed, blanched and diced
12 pickling onions, peeled
1 × 1½ kg (3 lb) roasting chicken, jointed
2 tablespoons brandy
1 bottled red Burgundy wine
salt
freshly ground black pepper
2 garlic cloves, peeled and crushed
1 bouquet garni
½ teaspoon ground nutmeg
225 g (8 oz) small button mushrooms
20 g (¾ oz) plain flour
1 teaspoon yeast extract (optional)

TO GARNISH:
heart-shaped fried croûtes
chopped fresh parsley

PREPARATION TIME: 40 minutes
COOKING TIME: 1½ hours
OVEN: 180°C, 350°F, Gas Mark 4

1 Melt 25 g (1 oz) of the butter in a flameproof casserole, add the bacon and onions and cook gently until the onions begin to colour. Transfer to a plate.

2 Add the chicken joints to the casserole and brown on all sides.

3 Warm the brandy, pour it over the chicken and set alight.

4 When the flames die down, return the bacon and onions to the casserole.

5 Heat the wine in a saucepan and pour it over the chicken. Season to taste with salt and pepper. Stir in the garlic, bouquet garni and nutmeg. Cover the casserole and cook in a preheated oven for 1 hour.

6 Stir in the mushrooms, re-cover and cook for a further 15 minutes. Remove the bouquet garni.

7 Mix the flour and the remaining butter to a paste and whisk into a sauce in small pieces. Bring just to the boil, stirring.

8 Stir in the yeast extract, if using; this deepens the colour, as red wine sauces tend to have an unappetizing 'greyness'. Adjust the seasoning, and serve garnished with croûtes and parsley.

CHICKEN VÉRONIQUE

4 chicken breasts, partly boned
salt
freshly ground black pepper
25 g (1 oz) butter
1 tablespoon oil
25 g (1 oz) plain flour
150 ml (¼ pint) medium white wine
150 ml (¼ pint) chicken stock
grated rind of ½ lemon
1 tablespoon lemon juice
1 bay leaf
150 ml (¼ pint) single cream
1 egg yolk
100 g (4 oz) green grapes, peeled, halved and seeded

TO GARNISH:
green grapes or kiwi fruit slices
watercress

PREPARATION TIME: 15 minutes
COOKING TIME: 55–60 minutes
OVEN: 180°C, 350°F, Gas Mark 4

1 Remove the skin from the chicken if liked, then sprinkle the pieces of chicken lightly with salt and pepper.

2 Heat the butter and oil in a pan, add the chicken and fry until lightly browned all over. Transfer to a casserole.

3 Stir the flour into the pan juices, then add the wine and stock and bring to the boil. Add the lemon rind and juice, with salt and pepper and pour over the chicken. Add the bay leaf.

4 Cover the casserole and cook in a preheated oven for about 40 minutes.

5 Blend the cream with the egg yolk, add some of the sauce from the casserole, then stir back into the casserole with the grapes. Replace the lid and return to the oven for 15 minutes.

6 Discard the bay leaf and serve garnished with small bunches of grapes or kiwi fruit slices and watercress.

Clockwise from top left: Chicken Marengo; Coq au Vin; Chicken Véronique

BEEF COBBLER

4 tablespoons oil
450 g (1 lb) stewing steak, trimmed and cut into
small cubes
1 tablespoon seasoned plain flour
2 onions, peeled and diced
2 carrots, peeled and diced
1 small turnip, peeled and diced
1 bay leaf
salt
freshly ground black pepper
450 ml (¾ pint) beef stock

SCONE TOPPING:
100 g (4 oz) self-raising flour
¼ teaspoon salt
50 g (2 oz) margarine
¼ teaspoon mixed herbs
1 egg
2 tablespoons milk

Clockwise from top:
Beef Cobbler;
Carbonnade de Boeuf;
Canard à l'Orange

PREPARATION TIME: 30 minutes
COOKING TIME: 1½ hours
OVEN: 180°C, 350°F, Gas Mark 4; then:
220°C, 425°F, Gas Mark 7

1 Heat 2 tablespoons of the oil in a frying pan or casserole. Toss the meat in the flour and fry on a fairly high heat until golden brown.

2 Turn down the heat, add the remaining oil and vegetables, and sauté gently for a few minutes. Add the bay leaf, seasoning and stock and bring to the boil.

3 Place in a casserole, if you have used a frying pan, cover and cook for 1 hour in a preheated oven.

4 Meanwhile, to make the scone topping, sieve the flour and salt, then rub in the fat until the mixture resembles fine breadcrumbs. Add the herbs and mix with the egg and milk to a soft dough. Roll out on a floured board 1 cm (½ inch) thick and cut into rounds or triangles.

5 Remove casserole from the oven, taste and adjust the seasoning. Turn up the heat and arrange the scones on top of the meat. Return the casserole uncovered to the second top shelf of the oven for 15 minutes or until the scone topping is golden brown.

CARBONNADE DE BOEUF

*750 g (1½ lb) braising steak, trimmed and cut into
5 cm (2 inch) slices
1 tablespoon plain flour
salt
freshly ground black pepper
50 g (2 oz) butter
1 tablespoon oil
50 g (2 oz) streaky bacon, rinded and diced
3 large onions, peeled and thinly sliced
300 ml (½ pint) brown ale
300 ml (½ pint) beef stock
1 teaspoon French mustard
bouquet garni
chopped fresh parsley
8 slices French bread
4 teaspoons French mustard*

PREPARATION TIME: 25 minutes
COOKING TIME: 1¾–2 hours
OVEN: 180°C, 350°F, Gas Mark 4

1 Toss the meat in seasoned flour until well coated. Reserve any remaining flour.

2 Melt the butter and oil in a frying pan, add the bacon and fry gently until browned. Transfer to a casserole.

3 Add the onions to the frying pan and sauté gently; then add the meat and brown on both sides. Transfer the onions and meat to the casserole.

4 Sprinkle the reserved flour into the pan, add the ale, stock and teaspoon of French mustard, and scrape the juices from the sides of the pan into the mixture. Stir together, season with salt and pepper, then pour over the meats in the casserole. Add the bouquet garni and parsley.

5 Put the covered casserole in a preheated oven and cook for 1½ hours or until tender.

6 Remove the bouquet garni, taste and adjust seasoning and consistency, if necessary. Place the slices of French bread, spread with mustard, on top of the meat and return the casserole, uncovered, to the oven for a further 15–20 minutes until the bread is golden brown.

CANARD À L'ORANGE

*25 g (1 oz) butter
1 × 1.75 kg (4 lb) duckling, quartered and trimmed
of fat
1 onion, peeled and finely chopped
300 ml (½ pint) giblet or chicken stock
2 cloves
2 oranges
juice of 1 lemon
salt
freshly ground black pepper
2 tablespoons Grand Marnier
1 teaspoon arrowroot
sprigs of parsley, to garnish*

PREPARATION TIME: 30 minutes
COOKING TIME: 1 hour 10 minutes
OVEN: 180°C, 350°F, Gas Mark 4

1 Melt the butter in a large frying pan, add the duckling quarters and brown well on all sides for about 10 minutes. Transfer to a casserole.

2 Pour off the surplus fat from the frying pan, leaving about 1 tablespoon. Stir in the onion and cook gently until softened. Add the stock, cloves and juice of 1 orange and the lemon and season to taste with salt and pepper.

3 Bring to the boil, then pour over the duckling. Cover the casserole and cook in a preheated oven for 1 hour, then skim off the fat.

4 Meanwhile, thinly peel the second orange (all white pith must be removed) and cut the rind into long, thin strips. Squeeze the juice and reserve.

5 Put the rind into a small saucepan, cover with cold water and bring to the boil. Simmer for 5 minutes, then drain. Stir the rind and the Grand Marnier into the casserole. Return the covered casserole to the oven and continue cooking for 7 minutes.

6 Arrange the duckling on a heated serving dish. Pour the sauce into a small saucepan and skim off the fat.

7 Dissolve the arrowroot in the reserved orange juice, add to the sauce and bring to the boil, stirring. Adjust the seasoning.

8 Pour the sauce over the duckling and serve garnished with the parsley.

BOEUF À LA MODE

SERVES 6
225 g (8 oz) fresh pork fat, cut into 20 cm (8 inch)
long, thin strips
⅛ teaspoon mixed spices
salt
freshly ground black pepper
120 ml (4 fl oz) cognac
2 tablespoons chopped fresh parsley
1½ kg (3½ lb) brisket, tied
2 tablespoons fresh thyme or 1 teaspoon dried thyme
1 bay leaf, crushed
1.2 litres (2 pints) dry white wine
2.75 litres (5 pints) water
2 calf's feet (or 4 pig's trotters), cut in half
50 g (2 oz) fresh pork rind
10 parsley sprigs
1 bay leaf
1 sprig fresh thyme
6 tablespoons butter
1 medium carrot, peeled and quartered
1 medium onion, peeled and quartered
5 garlic cloves, peeled
2.25 litres (4 pints) veal or beef stock

TO GARNISH:
20 small onions, peeled
1 tablespoon butter
450 g (1 lb) carrots, peeled and cut into thick strips

PREPARATION TIME: 1 hour, plus
marinating
COOKING TIME: 4 hours
OVEN: 160°C, 325°F, Gas Mark 3

Boeuf à la Mode can be served cold. Cut the meat into thin slices, and arrange in a shallow dish. Arrange the carrots, onions, calf's feet (if liked: they may be discarded, as their goodness has gone into the jelly) and rind around the slices. Pour over the sauce and chill overnight. If the sauce did not boil vigorously while cooking, it should set into a clear jelly.

1 Place the pork fat strips in a shallow container. Toss with the mixed spices, salt and pepper. Blend in 2 tablespoons of the cognac. Marinate for 30 minutes, turning the strips occasionally.

2 Sprinkle the pork fat strips with the parsley. With a larding needle, push the fat strips into the brisket in the direction of the grain of the meat. The strips should be evenly placed in the meat, forming a chequerboard pattern.

3 Season the brisket with the thyme, bay leaf, salt and pepper and place in a deep glass or ceramic bowl. Cover the meat with the white wine and remaining cognac. Cover and chill.

Marinate for at least 5 hours, preferably overnight, turning the meat occasionally.

4 Place the water in a large saucepan. Add the calf's feet and bring to the boil. Boil for 10 minutes, then remove the saucepan from the heat. Remove the meat from the water with a slotted spoon, then rinse under cold running water. Tie the feet in a piece of muslin cloth so they keep their shape and set aside. [A]

5 Bring the water in the saucepan to the boil again. Add the pork rind and cook for 5 minutes. Transfer the rind to a colander and rinse under cold running water. Tie the rind in a piece of muslin cloth, then set aside. [A]

6 Remove the meat from the marinade and wipe dry. Set aside.

7 Tie the parsley, thyme and bay leaf in a piece of muslin cloth to make a bouquet garni. [A]

8 Melt the butter in a large flameproof casserole over a medium heat. Add the meat, carrot and onion, then brown on all sides. Add the calf's feet, pork rind, bouquet garni and garlic. Blend in the marinade and stock. The meat should be completely covered. Bring just to the boil, skimming off the scum. Cover the casserole and cook in a preheated oven for 2 hours.

9 Just before removing the casserole from the oven, make the vegetable garnish. Melt the butter in a large frying pan over a moderate heat. Add the onions and brown on all sides.

10 Remove the casserole from the oven. Transfer the meat, the calf's feet and the pork rind to a heated platter. Discard the carrot and onion. Cut the feet and rind into 1 cm (½ inch) square pieces. Strain the sauce through a fine sieve, then allow to sit for 5 minutes. Remove the fat from the top of the sauce. Clean the casserole.

11 Return the meat, calf's feet, rind, onion and carrot garnish, and the stock to the cleaned casserole. Bring to the boil over a moderate heat, then cover. Transfer to a preheated oven and cook for 1 hour.

12 To serve, remove the string and slice the meat. Place it on a large heated serving platter. Surround with the calf's feet (if liked), rind, carrots and onions. Pour over just enough sauce to moisten. Serve the remaining sauce in a heated sauceboat.

[A] The calf's feet, pork rind and bouquet garni can be prepared earlier in the day, covered and kept chilled.

DAUBE DE BOEUF

SERVES 5–6

1 kg (2 lb) best braising steak in a piece, cut into
5 cm (2 inch) pieces
1 garlic clove, peeled and crushed
1 tablespoon chopped fresh parsley
1 teaspoon dried thyme
4 tablespoons brandy
150 ml (¼ pint) dry white wine
3 tablespoons oil
2 carrots, peeled and sliced
2 onions, peeled and sliced
450 ml (¾ pint) beef stock
salt
freshly ground black pepper
2-3 slices smoked cooked ham, diced
1 bay leaf
chopped fresh parsley, to garnish

PREPARATION TIME: 20 minutes, plus
marinating
COOKING TIME: about 3½ hours
OVEN: 150°C, 300°F, Gas Mark 2

1 Place the meat in a bowl. Add the garlic, parsley, thyme and brandy and mix well. Leave to stand for 15 minutes.

2 Add the wine, cover and leave to marinate for about 2 hours, turning the meat at least once.

3 Drain the meat, reserving the marinade. Heat the oil in a pan and fry the meat to seal, then place in a casserole.

4 Add the carrots and onions to the same fat and fry for 2 minutes. Add the marinade and stock and bring to the boil.

5 Add plenty of salt and pepper, the ham and bay leaf and pour into the casserole over the meat.

6 Cover tightly and cook in a preheated oven for about 3½ hours or until the beef is tender.

7 Discard the bay leaf, adjust the seasoning and serve sprinkled with chopped parsley.

Left: Boeuf à la Mode;
right: Daube de Boeuf

LANCASHIRE HOT POT

1 kg (2 lb) middle neck of lamb cutlets
3 tablespoons plain flour
salt
freshly ground black pepper
4 onions, peeled and finely sliced
2 lamb's kidneys, cored and sliced
225 g (8 oz) carrots, diced
750 g (1½ lb) potatoes, scrubbed and sliced
450 ml (¾ pint) light stock (bouillon)
1 bay leaf
½ teaspoon dried marjoram
½ teaspoon dried thyme

PREPARATION TIME: 25 minutes
COOKING TIME: 2½ hours
OVEN: 180°C, 350°F, Gas Mark 4

1 Trim any excess fat off the lamb and coat with the flour, seasoned with salt and pepper.

2 Place layers of meat, onions, kidneys, carrots and potatoes in a large casserole, seasoning each layer lightly with salt and pepper. Finish with a layer of potatoes.

3 Heat the stock and add the herbs. Pour into the casserole and cook, covered, in a preheated oven for 2 hours, until the meat is tender.

4 Remove the lid and cook for a further 30 minutes to brown the potatoes.

BOEUF BOURGUIGNON

SERVES 6
175 ml (6 fl oz) dry, red Burgundy wine
120 ml (4 fl oz) cognac
1½ kg (3 lb) braising steak, cubed
2.75 litres (5 pints) water
1 calf's foot, cut in half
50 g (2 oz) fresh pork rind
12 sprigs parsley
1 sprig fresh thyme
1 bay leaf
50 g (2 oz) butter
2 tablespoons plain flour
1.75 litres (3 pints) strong beef stock
450 g (1 lb) mushrooms, cleaned, quartered, stems removed and reserved
225 g (8 oz) bacon, rind removed and cut into strips
24 small onions, peeled

PREPARATION TIME: 45–60 minutes, plus marinating
COOKING TIME: 3¼ hours
OVEN: 160°C, 325°F, Gas Mark 3

Opposite, from the top:
Lancashire Hot Pot;
Boeuf Bourguignon;
Goulash

1 Combine the red wine and cognac in a large, shallow container. Add the beef, then toss well to coat all the pieces. Cover and marinate for 3 hours.

2 Bring 2.25 litres (4 pints) of the water to the boil in a large saucepan. Add the calf's foot and cook for 10 minutes. Remove the foot from the water and rinse under cold running water. Tie the foot in muslin cloth to retain its shape and set aside. [A]

3 Return the water to the boil. Add the pork rind and cook for 1 minute. Drain the rind and rinse under cold running water. Set aside. [A]

4 Tie the parsley, thyme and bay leaf in a piece of muslin cloth to make a bouquet garni. Set aside.

5 Remove the meat from the marinade and pat dry. Reserve the marinade.

6 Melt 2 tablespoons of the butter in a large flameproof casserole over a medium heat. Add the meat and brown on all sides. Remove the meat with a slotted spoon and set aside.

7 Using a whisk, stir the flour into the casserole. Cook for 2–3 minutes, stirring constantly. Gradually blend in the reserved marinade and stock. Bring to the boil and stir until smooth. Return the meat to the casserole. Add the bouquet garni, calf's foot, pork rind and the mushroom stems. Cover and cook in a preheated oven for 2 hours. [A]

8 While the casserole is cooking, bring the remaining water to the boil in a medium saucepan. Add the bacon pieces and boil for 1 minute. Drain in a colander.

9 Melt the remaining butter in a large frying pan over a moderate heat. Add the blanched bacon pieces, then cook for 10 minutes until browned. Remove the bacon pieces with a slotted spoon and drain on paper towels.

10 Add the onions to the frying pan. Cook for 10–15 minutes, until browned. Set aside.

11 Remove the casserole from the oven. Transfer the beef cubes to a heated platter. Remove the calf's foot and discard. Strain the sauce through a fine sieve. Clean the casserole dish. Return the beef to the casserole. Add the bacon, onions, mushrooms and sauce. Bring to the boil over a medium heat. Cover and transfer to a preheated oven. Cook the bourguignon for 30 minutes.

12 To serve, remove the beef, bacon, onions and mushroom caps with a slotted spoon. Place in a deep, heated platter. Pour the sauce over the boeuf bourguignon and serve immediately.

[A] The calf's foot and pork rind can be prepared in advance, covered and kept chilled. The casserole can be cooked in advance, then covered and kept chilled. Simmer for 15 minutes until heated through before proceeding.

GOULASH

2 tablespoons oil
450 g (1 lb) braising steak, trimmed and cubed
2 teaspoons paprika
2 teaspoons flour
300 ml (½ pint) stock
25 g (1 oz) butter
225 g (8 oz) onions, peeled and diced
225 g (8 oz) carrots, scrubbed and diced
1 bay leaf
good pinch of thyme
1 × 400 g (14 oz) can tomatoes
1 tablespoon tomato purée
1 teaspoon lemon juice
salt
freshly ground black pepper
1 potato, peeled and diced
8 small onions, peeled
1 tablespoon soured cream
finely chopped parsley, to garnish

PREPARATION TIME: 25–30 minutes
COOKING TIME: 1¾–2 hours
OVEN: 160°C, 325°F, Gas Mark 3

1 Heat the oil in a frying pan and fry the meat until brown on all sides. Reduce the heat, sprinkle with paprika and flour and turn the meat over to absorb the flour. After about 2–3 minutes pour the stock into the frying pan and stir gently. Pour the meat and stock into a casserole.

2 Rinse the pan, melt the butter and sweat the onions and carrots gently. Add the herbs, tomatoes, purée, lemon juice and seasoning. The potato can be made into balls or diced at this stage and added to the tomato mixture.

3 Pour the tomato mixture over the meat in the casserole and cook, covered, in a preheated oven for 1 hour. Add the onions and return for a further 45 minutes.

4 Before serving, remove the bay leaf, taste and adjust the seasoning, stir in the soured cream and sprinkle with parsley.

STEAK, KIDNEY AND MUSHROOM CASSEROLE

SERVES 4–6

*750 g (1½ lb) stewing or braising steak, cut into
2 cm (¾ inch) cubes
100-175 g (4-6 oz) ox kidney, chopped
1 tablespoon plain flour
1 large onion, peeled and thinly sliced
300 ml (½ pint) beef stock
1-2 tablespoons tomato purée
600 ml (1 pint) water
1 teaspoon Worcestershire sauce
salt
freshly ground black pepper
100 g (4 oz) mushrooms, sliced
1 tablespoon chopped fresh parsley, to garnish*

PREPARATION TIME: about 30 minutes
COOKING TIME: about 2¼ hours
OVEN: 160°C, 325°F, Gas Mark 3

Clockwise from left:
Steak, Kidney and
Mushroom Casserole;
Pot Roast Colonial
Goose; Oxtail Casserole

1 Place the steak and kidney in a bowl with the flour and toss until well coated, shaking off any excess flour.

2 Place the meat in a flameproof casserole and add the onion, stock, tomato purée and water and bring to the boil. Add the Worcestershire sauce and seasoning and cover the casserole. Place in a preheated oven and cook for 2 hours, or until the meat is tender.

3 Add the mushrooms at this stage, stirring them through the beef and returning the casserole to the oven to cook for a further 10–15 minutes.

4 Remove the casserole from the oven and serve garnished with the parsley.

POT ROAST COLONIAL GOOSE

SERVES 6
1 × 2 kg (4½ lb) leg of lamb, boned

STUFFING:
25 g (1 oz) butter or margarine
1 onion, peeled and finely chopped
2 sticks celery, finely chopped
3 rashers bacon, derinded and chopped
75 g (3 oz) cooked rice
pinch of ground allspice
salt
freshly ground black pepper
1 × 200 g (7 oz) can apricot halves
1 × 200 g (7 oz) can prunes
1 egg yolk

SAUCE:
150 ml (¼ pint) dry white wine
15 g (½ oz) melted butter
150 ml (¼ pint) beef stock
1½ tablespoons cornflour

TO GARNISH:
courgettes, lightly cooked
sprigs of fresh rosemary or parsley

PREPARATION TIME: 25 minutes, plus
marinating
COOKING TIME: about 2¼ hours
OVEN: 180°C, 350°F, Gas Mark 4

1 For the stuffing, melt the fat in a pan and fry the onion, celery and bacon until lightly browned. Place in a bowl with the cooked rice, allspice, salt and pepper.

2 Drain the apricots and prunes, reserving the juices. Chop about 4 apricots and 4 prunes and add to the stuffing; mix well and bind together with the egg yolk.

3 Use the stuffing to fill the bone cavity of the lamb and skewer or sew loosely back into shape, using a trussing needle and fine string.

4 Place the joint in a casserole with the wine, cover and leave to marinate for several hours, turning once.

5 Brush the surface of the meat with melted butter and sprinkle with salt. Cover and cook in the marinade in a preheated oven for about 2¼ hours or until tender and cooked through. Baste once or twice during cooking and remove the casserole lid for the last 20–30 minutes to brown the joint.

6 Strain off the juices into a saucepan, remove any fat from the surface and add 150 ml (¼ pint) mixed apricot and prune juice and the stock. Thicken with the cornflour blended in a little cold water and bring back to the boil for about 2 minutes. Serve in a sauceboat.

7 Remove the string or skewers from the lamb and place on a serving dish. Garnish with the remaining apricots, prunes and the courgettes, and sprigs of fresh rosemary or parsley.

OXTAIL CASSEROLE

2 tablespoons oil
2 oxtails, cut into 5 cm (2 inch) pieces
2 medium-sized onions, peeled and sliced
2 medium-sized carrots, peeled and sliced
1 clove garlic, peeled and crushed
2 tablespoons tomato purée
300 ml (½ pint) stock
150 ml (¼ pint) sherry
salt
freshly ground black pepper
bouquet garni
450 g (1 lb) button onions, peeled
25 g (1 oz) butter
100 g (4 oz) button mushrooms, washed

PREPARATION TIME: 20 minutes
COOKING TIME: 2½ hours
OVEN: 160°C, 325°F, Gas Mark 3

1 Heat the oil in a pan, add the oxtail and fry gently until browned. Remove to a casserole.

2 Add the vegetables (including the garlic) to the oil left in the pan and sauté gently until lightly browned. Remove the vegetables to the casserole, on top of the oxtail.

3 Blend together the tomato purée, stock and sherry and pour over the contents of the casserole. Season and add the bouquet garni. Cook in a preheated oven for 2 hours, or until the meat comes away from the bones.

4 Remove the bouquet garni and the meat from the casserole. Skim the fat from the cooled sauce. Return the meat to the casserole.

5 Sauté the onions in the butter for 10 minutes, add the mushrooms and cook for a further 10 minutes, then add both vegetables to the meat.

6 Simmer all the ingredients together for 10 minutes, taste and adjust the seasoning before serving.

BRAISED HAM

1 kg (2¼ lb) forelock or middle gammon
300 ml (½ pint) pale ale
freshly ground black pepper
2 tablespoons honey
4 tablespoons demerara sugar
1 teaspoon dry mustard
12 cloves

TO GARNISH:
orange wedges
watercress

PREPARATION TIME: 15 minutes, plus
soaking
COOKING TIME: 1 hour 10 minutes
OVEN: 180°C, 350°F, Gas Mark 4; then:
200°C, 400°F, Gas Mark 6

1 Soak the ham in cold water to cover for several hours. Drain, discarding the water.

2 Place the ham in a casserole with the pale ale, sprinkle with pepper and cook, covered, in a preheated oven for 40 minutes.

3 Remove the ham from the casserole and discard half the ale. Cut away the skin from the ham and score the fat diagonally.

4 Rub a mixture of the honey, sugar and dry mustard over the ham. Stud cloves into the ham surface in a diamond pattern and return the ham and half the ale to the casserole.

5 Cook, uncovered, at the higher temperature for a further 30 minutes, basting the joint every 10 minutes. Serve the ham garnished with wedges of orange and watercress.

JUGGED HARE

1 hare with blood
4 rashers streaky bacon, rinded
25 g (1 oz) butter
2 onions, peeled and finely chopped
2 carrots, peeled and finely diced
2 sticks celery, washed and thinly sliced
1 bay leaf
1 sprig parsley or ¼ teaspoon dried parsley
1 thyme sprig or ¼ teaspoon dried thyme
salt
freshly ground black pepper
1 litre (1¾ pints) stock
2 tablespoons redcurrant jelly
4 tablespoons port
sprigs thyme, to garnish

PREPARATION TIME: 25–30 minutes
COOKING TIME: 3½ hours
OVEN: 160°C, 325°F, Gas Mark 3

1 Joint the hare, retaining the blood.

2 Gently fry the streaky bacon in a frying pan until the fat runs out. Remove the bacon to a casserole and fry the joints of hare in the pan until golden brown; remove to the casserole.

3 Add the butter to the frying pan and cook the prepared vegetables gently for about 3–4 minutes. Add the vegetables to the hare in the casserole with the herbs and season well.

4 Boil up the stock in the frying pan and pour into the casserole, cover and cook in a preheated oven for 2½–3 hours, until the hare is tender.

5 Strain the gravy from the casserole and remove the hare on to a heated dish.

6 Return the gravy to the casserole, add the redcurrant jelly and port, bring to just under boiling point, simmer for a few minutes, taste and adjust the seasoning. Remove from the heat, gradually stir in the blood and reheat without allowing the sauce to boil. Strain the sauce over the hare and garnish with thyme.

CASSOULET

225 g (8 oz) dried white haricot beans, soaked in
water overnight
750 ml (1¼ pints) beef stock
100 g (4 oz) fresh pork rind, diced
8 garlic cloves, peeled
1 carrot, trimmed and lightly scraped
3 onions, peeled
4 cloves
2 tablespoons oil
100 g (4 oz) lean pork, cubed
100 g (4 oz) salt pork, cubed
350 g (12 oz) boned lamb shoulder, cubed
1 × 425 g (15 oz) can tomatoes with their juice
bouquet garni
salt
freshly ground black pepper
350 g (12 oz) garlic sausage or boiling ring, cut into
5 cm (2 inch) lengths
50 g (2 oz) fresh breadcrumbs
2 tablespoons chopped fresh parsley, to garnish

PREPARATION TIME: 1½ hours, plus
soaking
COOKING TIME: 3½ hours
OVEN: 170°C, 325°F, Gas Mark 3

1 Drain the soaked beans and put them into a large saucepan with the stock, pork rind, 4 whole garlic cloves, the carrot and 1 onion stuck with the cloves. Cover, bring slowly to the boil and simmer for 1 hour.

2 Strain off the liquid and reserve. Discard the carrot, onion and garlic. Put the beans and pork rind into a deep casserole.

3 Heat the oil in a large frying pan, add the pork, salt pork and lamb and brown on all sides. Lift out and add to the beans.

4 Thinly slice the remaining onions and fry gently in the fat until softened. Stir in the tomatoes, the remaining garlic, crushed, the bean cooking liquid, the bouquet garni and salt and pepper to taste.

5 Bring to the boil and pour over the beans. Mix all the ingredients well together, then cover the casserole and cook in a preheated oven for 2½ hours.

6 Remove the lid and carefully stir in the sausage pieces. Adjust the seasoning. Sprinkle the crumbs evenly over the top and return to the oven, uncovered. Cook for a further hour. The fat will rise to the surface to turn the crumbs into a crisp golden topping.

7 Do not allow the cassoulet to get too dry during the cooking; add a little more stock if necessary. The final dish should have a creamy consistency. Garnish the cassoulet with parsley before serving.

Clockwise from top right: Braised Ham; Jugged Hare; Cassoulet

CHOUCROÛTE GARNIE

SERVES 6

1¾ kg (4 lb) sauerkraut, rinsed and squeezed dry
freshly ground black pepper
2.25 litres (4 pints) water
225 g (8 oz) fresh pork fat, thinly sliced
12 parsley sprigs
1 sprig fresh thyme
1 bay leaf
12 juniper berries
1 large carrot, peeled and sliced
1 small onion, peeled, quartered and each quarter
studded with 1 clove
1 pig's trotter, about 225 g (8 oz)
450 g (1 lb) smoked bacon, rind removed
225 g (8 oz) sliced smoked ham
1 kg (2 lb) smoked pork loin
1 large garlic sausage, about 450 g (1 lb), pricked
475 g (16 fl oz) dry white wine
1.2 litres (2 pints) chicken stock
6 frankfurters, approx. 15–18 cm (6–7 inches)

PREPARATION TIME: 35 minutes
COOKING TIME: 3¾ hours
OVEN: 220°C, 425°F, Gas Mark 7

1 Spread the sauerkraut in a large, shallow container and grind the fresh, black pepper over it. Mix well, then set aside.

2 Bring 600 ml (1 pint) of the water to the boil in a medium saucepan. Add the pork fat slices and boil for 1 minute. Drain the slices, then rinse well under cold running water. Set aside.

3 Tie the parsley sprigs, thyme, bay leaf and juniper berries in a piece of muslin cloth to make a bouquet garni. Set aside.

4 Line the bottom and sides of a large flameproof casserole with the fat slices. Cover with ⅓ of the sauerkraut. Add ½ of the carrot, the onion, and the bouquet garni. Cover evenly with another ⅓ of the sauerkraut. Add the rest of the carrot and the pig's trotter. Top with the bacon, ham, pork loin and garlic sausage. Cover evenly with the remaining sauerkraut. Pour the white wine and stock into the casserole. [A]

5 Bring the casserole to the boil over a moderate heat. Top with a sheet of greaseproof paper, then cover. Place in a preheated oven and cook for 35 minutes.

6 Remove the casserole from the oven. Carefully remove the garlic sausage and set aside. Return the covered casserole to the oven. Cook for 1 hour.

7 After this time, remove the bacon and ham and set them aside. Return the covered casserole to the oven. Cook for 1½ hours.

8 Thirty minutes before the casserole is ready, bring the remaining water to the boil in a large saucepan. Lower the heat, then add the frankfurters. Cook for 10 minutes. Remove the frankfurters from the water and keep warm.

9 Remove the casserole from the oven. Remove the pork loin and slice. Keep warm. Top the sauerkraut with the sausage, bacon, ham and frankfurters. Cover and return to the oven. Cook for 15 minutes.

10 Remove the casserole from the oven. Transfer the bacon, ham, and frankfurters to a large plate. Remove the sausage and slice. Remove the pig's trotter and cut off the meat, discarding the skin and bone. Add the sausage and pig's trotter meat to the meats. Cover and keep warm. Remove the carrot slices and onion from the sauerkraut and discard. Stir the sauerkraut.

11 To serve, pile the sauerkraut in a dome on a long heated serving platter. Surround the sauerkraut with the ham slices, bacon slices, pig's trotter meat and pork loin slices. Surround the meats with the frankfurters. Serve with creamed potatoes.

[A] Can be prepared several hours in advance, covered and kept chilled. Allow to stand at room temperature for 30 minutes before proceeding with the recipe.

OSSO BUCCO

25 g (1 oz) butter
2 tablespoons olive oil
1 kg (2 lb) shin of veal, sawn into 4 equal pieces
1 onion, peeled and thinly sliced
450 g (1 lb) tomatoes, skinned and sliced, or
1 × 750 g (1 lb 10 oz) can tomatoes with their juice
1 garlic clove, peeled and crushed
150 ml (¼ pint) dry white wine
150 ml (¼ pint) veal or chicken stock
1 bay leaf
salt
freshly ground black pepper

GREMOLATA:
2 tablespoons chopped fresh parsley
1 garlic clove, peeled and finely chopped
grated rind of 1 small lemon

PREPARATION TIME: 30 minutes
COOKING TIME: about 2 hours

Opposite, from the top: Choucroûte Garni; Osso Bucco; Irish Stew

1 Melt the butter with the oil in a flameproof casserole, add the veal and brown on all sides. Transfer the veal to a warm plate.

2 Add the onion to the casserole and cook gently until soft and golden.

3 Stir in the tomatoes, with their juice if using canned tomatoes, the garlic and white wine. Allow to bubble for a few minutes, then return the meat to the casserole, with the stock and bay leaf. Season with salt and pepper.

4 Cover and simmer gently for 2 hours or until the meat is really tender and the sauce is rich and thick.

5 Meanwhile, mix together the parsley, garlic and lemon rind.

6 Serve the veal sprinkled with the gremolata, accompanied by risotto milanese (rice cooked with white wine, saffron and beef marrow).

IRISH STEW

2 large onions, peeled and sliced
1 kg (2 lb) scrag end of neck of lamb, cut into slices
2 teaspoons mixed dried herbs (optional)
salt
freshly ground black pepper
2-3 large potatoes, peeled and sliced
600 ml (1 pint) stock or water
1 tablespoon finely chopped fresh parsley, to garnish

PREPARATION TIME: 15 minutes
COOKING TIME: 1½ hours
OVEN: 180°C, 350°F, Gas Mark 4

1 Place a third to a half of the onions in a casserole and put the lamb on top.

2 Sprinkle in the herbs, if using, and season well with salt and pepper.

3 Add the remaining onions and the sliced potatoes, mixed, and season well.

4 Pour over the stock.

5 Put the casserole, covered, in a preheated oven and cook for 1¼ hours. Remove the lid and cook for a further 15 minutes to allow the top to brown slightly.

6 Sprinkle the Irish stew with parsley and serve accompanied by colourful vegetables such as peas and carrots.

NEW ENGLAND BEEF DINNER

1 × 1½ kg (3½ lb) joint salt brisket of beef
1 bay leaf, parsley stalks, sprig of fresh thyme
(or 1 bouquet garni)
1 teaspoon black peppercorns
4 cloves
1 onion, peeled
8 carrots, scraped and halved lengthways
8 small potatoes, peeled and halved
1 small, tight cabbage, quartered and cored
chopped fresh parsley, to garnish

PREPARATION TIME: 20 minutes
COOKING TIME: 3½–4 hours

1 Put the brisket into a deep flameproof casserole, cover with cold water and add the herbs or bouquet garni and peppercorns.

2 Stick the cloves into the onion and add to the pot. Cover and bring very slowly to the boil, skimming off the scum. Simmer very gently for 3 hours.

3 Add the carrots and potatoes, re-cover and continue simmering for 20 minutes.

4 Stir in the cabbage, re-cover and cook for a further 20–30 minutes or until the meat and vegetables are tender.

5 Remove the meat to a board, slice it and arrange the slices on a heated serving dish. Surround with the drained vegetables.

6 Strain the broth, adjust the seasoning and pour a little over the meat; serve the remainder separately.

7 Sprinkle with chopped parsley. Serve with plenty of fresh, crusty bread.

PAUPIETTES DE VEAU

SERVES 6

FOR THE SAUCE:
225 g (8 oz) bacon, rinded and cut into strips
15 g (½ oz) butter
3 large tomatoes, peeled, seeded and diced
2 medium carrots, peeled and sliced
1 large onion, peeled and sliced
4 tablespoons plain flour
750 ml (1¼ pints) strong beef stock
120 ml (4 fl oz) Madeira wine
1 tablespoon fresh thyme leaves or ½ teaspoon dried thyme
1 bay leaf, crushed
salt
freshly ground black pepper

FOR THE VEAL:
8 × 50 g (2 oz) veal escalopes
100 g (4 oz) Parma ham, cut to fit the escalopes
8 fresh sage leaves
salt
freshly ground black pepper
1 tablespoon butter
1 tablespoon oil
1 bunch watercress, to garnish

PREPARATION TIME: 30 minutes
COOKING TIME: 1½ hours
OVEN: 180°C, 350°F, Gas Mark 4

1 For the sauce, place the bacon pieces in a large saucepan over a moderate heat. Cook, stirring frequently, for 10 minutes until crisp. Remove the bacon with a slotted spoon and drain on paper towels. Set aside. [A]

2 Melt the butter in the saucepan and add the tomatoes, carrots and onion. Cook for 10 minutes until the onion is soft and golden. Blend in the flour then, stirring constantly, cook for 2–3 minutes. Using a whisk, gradually stir in the stock and Madeira. Bring to the boil, stirring constantly. Simmer for 5 minutes until smooth and thick. Add the thyme, bay leaf, salt and pepper. Remove from the heat and stir the bacon pieces. Set aside. [A]

3 For the veal, place the escalopes on a working surface. Place 1 slice of the Parma ham on each escalope. Top each with 1 sage leaf. Roll up the escalopes and secure with metal skewers or wooden toothpicks. Season each escalope with salt and pepper and set aside. [A]

4 Heat the butter and oil in a large flameproof casserole. Add the escalopes and brown on all sides for 5 minutes, turning occasionally. Drain

off the excess fat and discard. Coat the escalopes with the sauce, cover and place in a preheated oven. Cook for 45 minutes.

5 To serve, place the escalopes on a heated platter. Taste the sauce and adjust the seasoning, if necessary, then pour over the escalopes. Serve immediately, garnished with watercress.

[A] The bacon and the sauce can be made a day in advance, covered and kept chilled. Bring the sauce to the boil before proceeding with the recipe. The escalopes can be filled with the Parma ham and sage earlier in the day, then covered and kept chilled.

Top: New England Beef Dinner; bottom: Paupiettes de Veau

CALAMARES EN SU TINTA
(Squid in Its Own Ink)

1 kg (2 lb) squids with ink sacs
2 × 2.5 cm (1 inch) slices French bread
120 ml (4 fl oz) water
100 g (4 oz) whole blanched almonds, finely chopped
6 garlic cloves, peeled and finely chopped
2 tablespoons finely chopped fresh parsley
85 ml (3 fl oz) olive oil
450 ml (¾ pint) dry white wine
250 ml (8 fl oz) fish stock
salt
freshly ground black pepper

PREPARATION TIME: 45 minutes, plus standing
COOKING TIME: 1 hour

1 To clean the squid, separate the head – to which the tentacles are attached – from the body by pulling it out. Remove the pen (the rudimentary skeleton). Cut the tentacles off, then discard the pen and head. Clean the tentacles under running water and set aside. When the head is pulled out from the body, the fragile ink sac will be visible inside the body. Gently remove the ink sac and place in a medium bowl. Repeat for the remaining squid. Cover the ink sacs with water and set aside.

2 Remove the mantle – the purplish skin – by carefully peeling it away from the body. Turn the body inside out and clean well under running water. Turn the body back. Repeat for the remaining squid. Cut the squid into bite-sized pieces.

3 Place the bread in the water and soak for 15 minutes, turning occasionally. Squeeze the bread dry.

4 In a food processor or using a pestle and mortar, liquidize the bread, almonds, garlic and parsley to a paste.

5 Heat the oil in a flameproof casserole over a medium-high heat. Add the paste and cook for 2 minutes, stirring constantly. Stir in the squids, tentacles, wine, stock, salt and pepper. Cover and simmer for 45 minutes, stirring occasionally.

6 Carefully drain the ink sacs. Crush the ink sacs and collect the ink in a bowl. Stir into the casserole and bring the mixture to the boil. Cook for 10 minutes, stirring occasionally. Taste the casserole and correct the seasoning, if necessary. Serve immediately with boiled rice.

SOLE AND PRAWN PAUPIETTES

8 lemon sole fillets, skinned
2 tablespoons lemon juice
175 g (6 oz) cooked, peeled prawns
salt
freshly ground black pepper
150 ml (¼ pint) milk
150 ml (¼ pint) fish stock
1 bay leaf
2 sprigs fresh parsley
1 teaspoon butter, for greasing

FOR THE SAUCE:
25 g (1 oz) butter
25 g (1 oz) plain flour
150 ml (¼ pint) milk
2 teaspoons anchovy essence
4 sprigs fresh parsley, to garnish

PREPARATION TIME: 15 minutes
COOKING TIME: 30 minutes
OVEN: 180°C, 350°F, Gas Mark 4

1 Lay the sole fillets, skinned side up, on a working surface. Sprinkle with lemon juice.

2 Set aside 8 of the prawns for the garnish and chop the remainder. Put a little of the chopped prawns on each sole fillet. Season with the salt and pepper. Roll up tightly from the tail end and secure with a wooden cocktail stick. Place the fillets in a small casserole. [A]

3 Combine the milk and fish stock in a small bowl. Pour over the fillets, then add the bay leaf and parsley sprigs. Cover the casserole with a sheet of greaseproof paper, greased with the teaspoon of butter, and the lid. Place in a preheated oven and cook for 15–20 minutes, until the paupiettes are firm to the touch.

4 Remove the casserole from the oven. Transfer the fillets to a heated serving platter and keep warm. Strain the cooking liquid, discarding the bay leaf and parsley, and reserve.

5 Melt the butter in a medium saucepan over a moderate heat. Blend in the flour and cook for 2–3 minutes, stirring frequently. Using a whisk, gradually stir in the reserved liquid, milk and anchovy essence. Bring to the boil and simmer for 2 minutes, until thick and smooth. Taste and correct seasoning, if necessary, then remove from the heat. To serve, pour the sauce over the sole and garnish with the parsley and reserved prawns.

[A] Can be prepared 2 hours in advance, covered and kept chilled.

SEAFOOD CASSEROLE

SERVES 6

450 g (1 lb) haddock or cod fillet, skinned
225 g (8 oz) smoked haddock fillet, skinned
100 g (4 oz) peeled prawns
3-4 scallops, quartered or 1 × 150 g (5 oz) jar
mussels, drained
1 × 300 g (11 oz) can sweetcorn kernels, drained
(optional)
1-2 canned red pimentos, sliced (optional)
40 g (1½ oz) butter or margarine
40 g (1½ oz) plain flour
300 ml (½ pint) milk
1 teaspoon made English mustard
1 tablespoon lemon juice
4 tablespoons soured cream
salt
freshly ground black pepper
whole prawns, to garnish

PREPARATION TIME: 10 minutes
COOKING TIME: 40–45 minutes
OVEN: 180°C, 350°F, Gas Mark 4

1 Cut the white and smoked fish into 2.5 cm (1 inch) cubes. Place in a large, fairly shallow casserole with the prawns, scallops or mussels, sweetcorn and pimentos (if using).

2 Melt the butter or margarine in a pan, stir in the flour and cook for 1 minute. Gradually add the milk and bring slowly to the boil.

3 Stir the mustard, lemon juice, soured cream and plenty of salt and pepper into the sauce and pour into the casserole.

4 Cook in a preheated oven for about 40 minutes or until the fish is cooked through.

5 Give the casserole a gentle stir before serving garnished with whole prawns.

From the left: Calamares en su Tinta; Sole and Prawn Paupiettes; Seafood Casserole

VEGETARIAN DISHES

Imaginative combinations of vegetables and
pulses and clever use of flavourings and toppings
give good variety to the recipes in this chapter.
Here are hearty main meals such as Vegetable
Goulash and Winter Vegetable Hot Pot, lighter
dishes for lunch or supper such as Courgette and
Brown Rice Layered Casserole or Lentil-Stuffed
Courgettes, and some tasty accompanying dishes
like Baked Lemon Carrots and Pommes
Dauphinoises which non-vegetarians could serve
with many of the meat, poultry and fish
casseroles in other chapters. The carefully-
planned protein content of many of the vegetable
casseroles ensures that, served perhaps with rice
and a salad, they would be nutritious and
satisfying main meals for non-meat eaters.

LENTIL-STUFFED COURGETTES

2 tablespoons oil
1 onion, peeled and chopped
100 g (4 oz) mushrooms, peeled and chopped
2 sticks celery, sliced
225 g (8 oz) small brown Continental lentils, soaked overnight
600 ml (1 pint) water
salt
freshly ground black pepper
4 large courgettes, wiped
2 teaspoons cornflour

PREPARATION TIME: 15 minutes, plus soaking
COOKING TIME: 1 hour–1 hour 10 minutes
OVEN: 180°C, 350°F, Gas Mark 4

1 Heat the oil in a pan, add the onion, mushrooms and celery and cook for 2–3 minutes. Add the lentils and water to the pan, bring to the boil, cover the pan and cook for 20–30 minutes until the lentils are tender, then add salt and pepper. Drain well, reserving the cooking liquid. [A]

2 Cut the ends off each courgette and cut each one diagonally into pieces about 7.5 cm (3 inches) long. Scoop out the seeds. Stuff the courgette pieces with the lentil mixture.

3 Put the courgettes into a casserole, pour over the reserved cooking liquid, cover the casserole and put into a preheated oven. Cook for about 40 minutes, until the courgettes are tender.

4 When the courgettes are cooked, remove them from the casserole, arrange them on a warmed serving dish and keep them warm.

5 Pour the cooking liquid into a small saucepan and make up about 300 ml (½ pint) with water, if necessary. Mix the cornflour with a little cold water, add to the saucepan, bring to the boil, then pour the sauce over the courgettes.

[A] The lentils and vegetables can be cooked up to 1 day in advance. Keep covered and chilled.

Variation: One medium-size marrow may be used instead of the courgettes. Cut the ends off the marrow, scoop out the fibres and seeds, stuff with the lentil mixture and put the ends back on the marrow, securing them in place with cocktail sticks. Cook the marrow in a casserole, as for the courgettes, for about 1 hour, turning the marrow in the cooking liquid. The stuffed marrow may be served sliced.

CHINESE VEGETABLE CASSEROLE

25 g (1 oz) dried Chinese mushrooms, soaked for 15 minutes in boiling water
2 tablespoons oil
1 onion, peeled and sliced
2 teaspoons cornflour
1 tablespoon light soy sauce
300 ml (½ pint) vegetable stock
½ teaspoon five spice powder
225 g (8 oz) whole baby sweetcorn
100 g (4 oz) bean sprouts
1 × 225 g (8 oz) can bamboo shoots, drained
salt
freshly ground black pepper
100 g (4 oz) mangetout, topped and tailed

PREPARATION TIME: 15 minutes, plus soaking
COOKING TIME: 40 minutes
OVEN: 180°C, 350°F, Gas Mark 4

1 Drain the Chinese mushrooms, discard the stalks then chop roughly.

2 Heat the oil in a flameproof casserole, add the onion and cook until soft.

3 Mix together the cornflour, soy sauce, stock and five spice powder then add to the casserole. Add the mushrooms, sweetcorn, bean sprouts and bamboo shoots. Bring to the boil, taste and adjust the seasoning, if necessary, then cover the casserole, put into a preheated oven and cook for 10 minutes.

4 Add the mangetout to the casserole and cook for a further 10 minutes.

TOMATO, SPINACH AND RICOTTA CHEESE CASSEROLE

750 g (1½ lb) spinach, washed and shredded
1 tablespoon water
salt
25 g (1 oz) butter
1 onion, peeled and chopped
1 garlic clove, peeled and crushed
4 large tomatoes, peeled and sliced
350 g (12 oz) ricotta cheese
freshly ground black pepper
1 tablespoon grated Parmesan cheese

PREPARATION TIME: 15 minutes
COOKING TIME: 50 minutes
OVEN: 180°C, 350°F, Gas Mark 4

1 Put the spinach in a pan with the water and a little salt. Cook for 2–3 minutes until soft, then drain well.

2 Use a little of the butter to grease a casserole. Melt the remaining butter in a pan, add the onion and garlic and cook until soft, stir into the spinach and mix well.

3 Put half the spinach, two of the tomatoes and half the ricotta cheese in layers in the casserole. Repeat the layers, seasoning between each layer. Sprinkle with the Parmesan cheese.

4 Cover the casserole and put into a preheated oven. Cook for 30 minutes, uncover the casserole and cook for a further 10 minutes to brown the top.

Clockwise from top right: Chinese Vegetable Casserole; Lentil-Stuffed Courgettes; Tomato, Spinach and Ricotta Cheese Casserole

AUBERGINES STUFFED WITH PINE NUTS

2 large aubergines, about 350 g (12 oz) each
salt
25 g (1 oz) butter
1 large onion, peeled and chopped
1 garlic clove, peeled and crushed
50 g (2 oz) pine nuts
4 large tomatoes, peeled, seeded and chopped
1 tablespoon tomato purée
1 teaspoon dried oregano
2 teaspoons paprika
freshly ground black pepper
50 ml (¼ pint) vegetable stock

PREPARATION TIME: 20 minutes, plus salting
COOKING TIME: 1 hour–1 hour 10 minutes
OVEN: 180°C, 350°F, Gas Mark 4

1 Remove the stalks from the aubergines, cut the aubergines in half lengthways, then cut each half into three slices, lengthways. Put the slices into a colander, sprinkle with salt, and leave for 30 minutes to drain.

2 While the aubergines are draining, make the filling. Melt the butter in a pan, add the onion and garlic and cook until soft. Add the pine nuts and stir around until lightly browned.

3 Add the tomatoes, tomato purée, oregano, paprika and pepper to the pan. Stir well and cook until a thick purée is formed.

4 Rinse the aubergine slices in cold water and dry on paper towels. Heat the oil in a frying pan and fry the aubergine slices a few at a time for about 1 minute each side. Drain the aubergine on paper towels.

5 Reassemble the aubergine halves by spreading about 1 tablespoon of the filling between each slice and pressing the slices together. [A]

6 Put the aubergine halves into a shallow casserole. Pour the stock over, cover the casserole and cook for 45–50 minutes.

[A] The aubergines can be prepared up to 1 day in advance. Keep covered and chilled.

CHICK PEA AND CAULIFLOWER CURRY

175 g (6 oz) chick peas, soaked overnight
3–4 tablespoons oil
1 onion, peeled and chopped
1 garlic clove, peeled and crushed
175 g (6 oz) carrots, peeled and diced
225 g (8 oz) cauliflower florets
2 teaspoons ground turmeric
1 teaspoon ground cumin
½ teaspoon ground coriander
½ teaspoon ground ginger
½ teaspoon garam masala
½ teaspoon ground chilli
salt
freshly ground black pepper
1 large potato, peeled and diced

PREPARATION TIME: 20 minutes, plus soaking
COOKING TIME: 2 hours
OVEN: 180°C, 350°F, Gas Mark 4

1 Put the chick peas into a saucepan. Cover with cold water, bring to the boil and boil rapidly for 10 minutes. Reduce the heat and cook for a further 30–40 minutes, until tender.

[A] Drain the chick peas, reserving 350 ml (12 fl oz) of the cooking water. Put the chick peas into a casserole.

2 Heat the oil in a pan, add the onion and garlic and cook until soft, then add to the casserole. Add the carrots and cauliflower to the pan, cook until lightly browned then transfer them to the casserole.

3 Put the spices into the pan, adding a little extra oil, if necessary. Cook the spices gently for 1 minute, then add the reserved liquid, salt, pepper and potato. Bring to the boil, pour into the casserole, stir well, then cover the casserole, place in a preheated oven and cook for 1–1¼ hours, stirring from time to time. [F]

[A] The chick peas can be cooked up to 1 day in advance. Keep covered and chilled.

[F] Freeze for up to 3 months. Defrost at room temperature for 4–6 hours or overnight in the refrigerator. Reheat for 30 minutes at 180°C, 350°F, Gas Mark 4.

SPICED RED CABBAGE AND BEETROOT CASSEROLE WITH CHESTNUTS

50 g (2 oz) butter
1 large onion, peeled and sliced
450 g (1 lb) red cabbage, washed, quartered and shredded
225 g (8 oz) cooking apple, peeled, cored and chopped
350 g (12 oz) peeled weight chestnuts or 275 g (10 oz) canned whole chestnuts
2 tablespoons soft brown sugar
1 tablespoon red wine vinegar
½ teaspoon ground nutmeg
½ teaspoon ground cinnamon
300 ml (½ pint) water
salt
freshly ground black pepper
225 g (8 oz) fresh cooked beetroot, peeled and chopped

PREPARATION TIME: 20 minutes
COOKING TIME: 1 hour 20 minutes
OVEN: 180°C, 350°F, Gas Mark 4

1 Melt the butter in a flameproof casserole, add the onion and cook until soft. Add the red cabbage and apple and stir well together until the cabbage is coated with the butter.

2 Add the chestnuts, brown sugar, vinegar, spices, water, salt and pepper to the casserole and stir well. Bring to the boil, cover the casserole, put into a preheated oven and cook for 1 hour until the chestnuts are cooked.

3 Add the beetroot to the casserole and cook for a further 15 minutes. [F]

[F] Freeze for up to 3 months. Defrost for 4–6 hours at room temperature or overnight in a refrigerator. Reheat for 30 minutes at 180°C, 350°F, Gas Mark 4.

Clockwise from top left: Chick Pea and Cauliflower Curry; Spiced Red Cabbage and Beetroot Casserole with Chestnuts; Aubergines Stuffed with Pine Nuts

BAKED RATATOUILLE WITH GOAT'S CHEESE CROÛTES

2 tablespoons olive oil
1 large onion, peeled and sliced
2 garlic cloves, peeled and crushed
1 red pepper, cored, seeded and sliced
1 green pepper, cored, seeded and sliced
225 g (8 oz) aubergine, stalk removed and diced
225 g (8 oz) courgettes, topped, tailed and sliced
1 × 400 g (14 oz) can chopped tomatoes
2 teaspoons Herbes de Provence
salt
freshly ground black pepper
1 small French loaf
2-3 tablespoons oil
175-225 g (6-8 oz) goat's cheese, cut into 8

PREPARATION TIME: 20 minutes
COOKING TIME: 1 hour 20 minutes
OVEN: 180°C, 350°F, Gas Mark 4

1 Heat the oil in a flameproof casserole, add the onion and garlic and cook until soft. Add the peppers, aubergine and courgettes to the casserole and mix well, then add the tomatoes and juice, Herbes de Provence, salt and pepper. Bring to the boil, cover the casserole and put into a preheated oven and cook for 1 hour. [A] [F]

2 After the casserole has been in the oven for 45 minutes, cut the French loaf into 8 slices, about 2.5–3 cm (1–1½ inches) wide, discarding the ends.

3 Dip each slice of the French bread into the oil, place on a baking sheet and put into the oven above the casserole for 15 minutes until crisp.

4 Take the casserole from the oven, remove the lid, stir the vegetables, then put the slices of bread on top of the vegetables. Put a piece of goat's cheese on top of each piece of French bread. Put under a preheated hot grill until the cheese is bubbling.

[A] The ratatouille can be prepared 1 day in advance. Keep covered and chilled, then proceed with the recipe.

[F] Freeze for up to 3 months. Defrost for 4–6 hours at room temperature or overnight in a refrigerator. Reheat for 30 minutes at 180°C, 350°F, Gas Mark 4.

From the top: Baked Ratatouille wtih Goat's Cheese Croûtes; Chicory Casserole with Toasted Walnuts; Courgette and Brown Rice Layered Casserole

CHICORY CASSEROLE WITH TOASTED WALNUTS

*8 small, even-sized heads of chicory, approx 100 g
(4 oz) each
1 tablespoon lemon juice
salt
25 g (1 oz) butter
1 small onion, peeled and finely chopped
1 tablespoon plain flour
85 ml (3 fl oz) milk
150 ml (5 fl oz) vegetable stock
freshly ground black pepper
1 tablespoon lemon juice
50 g (2 oz) chopped walnuts*

PREPARATION TIME: 15 minutes
COOKING TIME: 1 hour–1 hour 10 minutes
OVEN: 180°C, 350°F, Gas Mark 4

1 Remove the core from the base of each chicory head and discard. Put the chicory into a pan of boiling salted water with the lemon juice and cook for 5 minutes. (The lemon juice prevents the chicory heads turning brown when cooked.) Drain well, then put into a shallow casserole.

2 Melt the butter in a pan, add the onion and cook for 2 minutes. Stir in the flour and cook for a further minute. Add the milk and vegetable stock to the pan, bring to the boil and cook for 2–3 minutes. Add the pepper and lemon juice, then pour over the chicory.

3 Cover the casserole and cook for 30–40 minutes, until the chicory is tender.

4 Put the walnuts on to a baking sheet and put them into the oven at the same time as the chicory, taking them out again after about 10 minutes.

5 Serve the chicory sprinkled with the toasted walnuts.

COURGETTE AND BROWN RICE LAYERED CASSEROLE

*2 tablespoons oil
1 onion, peeled and chopped
1 garlic clove, peeled and crushed
225 g (8 oz) tomatoes, peeled, seeded and chopped
450 g (1 lb) courgettes, topped, tailed and thinly
sliced
½ teaspoon dried tarragon
salt
freshly ground black pepper
450 g (1 lb) cooked brown rice
2 eggs, beaten
150 ml (5 fl oz) double or whipping cream
100 g (4 oz) grated Cheddar cheese*

PREPARATION TIME: 20 minutes
COOKING TIME: 50 minutes
OVEN: 180°C, 350°F, Gas Mark 4

1 Heat the oil in a pan, add the onion and garlic and cook until soft. Add the tomatoes, courgettes, tarragon, salt and pepper and cook for a further 3–4 minutes. [A]

2 Mix together the rice, eggs, cream, most of the cheese and a little salt and pepper. [A]

3 Put a third of the rice mixture into a casserole followed by half of the courgette mixture. Repeat the layers, then finish with a layer of rice. Sprinkle the remaining cheese over the top. Put into a preheated oven and cook for 40 minutes.

[A] The courgettes and rice can be prepared up to 8 hours in advance, then proceed with the recipe.

FENNEL PARMIGIANO

750 g (1½ lb) fennel
salt
2 tablespoons olive oil
1 large onion, peeled and chopped
1 garlic clove, peeled and crushed
1 teaspoon chopped fresh basil or ½ teaspoon dried basil
freshly ground black pepper
175 g (6 oz) Mozarella cheese, sliced
25 g (1 oz) freshly grated Parmesan cheese
15 g (½ oz) butter

TO GARNISH:
fennel leaves
tomato wedges

PREPARATION TIME: 15 minutes
COOKING TIME: 45 minutes
OVEN: 190°C, 375°F, Gas Mark 5

From the left: Fennel Parmigiano; Vegetable Goulash; Aduki Bean and Bulghar Casserole

1 Dice the fennel, discarding the core and reserving the leaves for garnish. Put the fennel into a pan of cold salted water, bring to the boil, then drain and discard all but 2 tablespoons of the water.

2 Heat the olive oil in a pan, add the onion and garlic and cook until soft.

3 Put the fennel into a shallow casserole, stir in the oil, onion, garlic, basil, pepper and reserved water. Stir well.

4 Lay the slices of Mozarella cheese over the top of the fennel, then sprinkle with the Parmesan cheese.

5 Dot with the butter, put uncovered into a preheated oven and cook for 35 minutes.

6 Garnish with the reserved fennel leaves and wedges of tomato.

VEGETABLE GOULASH

2 tablespoons oil
1 large onion, peeled and chopped
1 tablespoon paprika
1 × 400 g (14 oz) can tomatoes
1 large green pepper, cored, seeded and chopped
225 g (8 oz) peeled weight carrots, sliced
225 g (8 oz) peeled weight potatoes, diced
225 g (8 oz) peeled weight pumpkin or squash, diced
salt
freshly ground black pepper
150 ml (5 fl oz) soured cream

PREPARATION TIME: 20 minutes
COOKING TIME: 1 hour 10 minutes–1 hour
25 minutes
OVEN: 180°C, 350°F, Gas Mark 4

1 Heat the oil in a flameproof casserole, add the onion and cook until soft, then add the paprika and cook for 1 minute. Add the tomatoes and their juice, then bring to the boil.

2 Add the green pepper, carrots, potatoes and pumpkin to the casserole and season with the salt and pepper.

3 Cover the casserole, put into a preheated oven and cook for 1–1¼ hours, stirring from time to time. [F]

4 Put the casserole back on to the heat. Stir in most of the soured cream and reheat gently without boiling. Put the remaining soured cream on top of the casserole before serving.

[F] Freeze for up to 3 months. Defrost for 4–6 hours at room temperature or overnight in a refrigerator. Reheat for 30 minutes at 180°C, 350°F, Gas Mark 4, then proceed as in the recipe.

ADUKI BEAN AND BULGHAR CASSEROLE

225 g (8 oz) aduki beans, soaked overnight
2 tablespoons oil
1 onion, peeled and chopped
1 garlic clove, peeled and crushed
225 g (8 oz) carrots, peeled and diced
1 green pepper, cored, seeded and diced
1 tablespoon tomato purée
300 ml (½ pint) vegetable stock
175 g (6 oz) bulghar, soaked for 30 minutes
salt
freshly ground black pepper
50 g (2 oz) melted butter
3 tablespoons boiling water

PREPARATION TIME: 20 minutes, plus
soaking
COOKING TIME: 1½ hours
OVEN: 180°C, 350°F, Gas Mark 4

1 Put the beans into a pan of cold water, bring to the boil, boil rapidly for 10 minutes, then reduce the heat and cook for a further 15 minutes or until soft. Drain the beans and set aside. [A]

2 Heat the oil in a pan, add the onion, garlic, carrots and green pepper and cook for 3 minutes.

3 Put the drained beans into a casserole, add the vegetables, tomato purée, stock, half the bulghar, salt and pepper and mix well.

4 Mix the remaining bulghar with the melted butter and water and put in an even layer over the beans and vegetables. Cook the casserole, uncovered, in a preheated oven for 1 hour.

[A] The beans can be cooked up to 1 day in advance. Keep covered and chilled.

BLACK-EYE BEAN STROGANOFF

350 g (12 oz) black-eye beans, soaked overnight
2 tablespoons oil
1 large onion, peeled and sliced
1 garlic clove, peeled and crushed
350 g (12 oz) mushrooms, peeled and sliced
2 teaspoons paprika
1 tablespoon tomato purée
150 ml (¼ pint) vegetable stock
salt
freshly ground black pepper
150 ml (5 fl oz) soured cream
paprika, to garnish

PREPARATION TIME: 15 minutes, plus
soaking
COOKING TIME: 1¼ hours
OVEN: 180°C, 350°F, Gas Mark 4

Black-Eye Bean
Stroganoff

1 Put the beans into a pan of cold water, bring to the boil and boil rapidly for 10 minutes. Reduce the heat and simmer for 20–30 minutes. The beans should be cooked but still firm. [A]

2 While the beans are cooking, heat the oil in a pan, then fry the onion, garlic and mushrooms for 2–3 minutes. Add the paprika to the pan and cook for a further minute.

3 Drain the beans and put into a casserole. Add the onion, garlic and mushrooms, the tomato purée, stock, salt and pepper to the casserole. Stir well, cover the casserole, put into a preheated oven and cook for 40 minutes.

4 Remove the casserole from the oven. Swirl in the soured cream and sprinkle with paprika.

[A] The beans can be cooked up to 1 day in advance. Keep covered and chilled.

BOSTON BAKED BEANS

350 g (12 oz) haricot beans, soaked overnight
3 tablespoons oil
1 onion, peeled and chopped
1 garlic clove, peeled and crushed
1 tablespoon wholegrain mustard
1 tablespoon molasses or black treacle
1 × 150 g (5 oz) can tomato purée
1 tablespoon soft brown sugar
salt
freshly ground black pepper

PREPARATION TIME: 10 minutes, plus
soaking
COOKING TIME: 4¾ hours
OVEN: 140°C, 275°F, Gas Mark 1

1 Put the beans into a pan, cover with cold water, bring to the boil and boil rapidly for 10 minutes. Reduce the heat and simmer for a further 30 minutes. Drain the beans, reserving 600 ml (1 pint) of the cooking liquid. [A]

2 Heat the oil in a pan, add the onion and garlic and cook until lightly browned.

3 Put the beans into a casserole, add the onion and garlic and any remaining oil, then add the mustard, molasses or treacle, tomato purée, sugar, salt and pepper. Mix in the reserved cooking liquid.

4 Cover the casserole with foil and a lid, place in a preheated oven and cook for 4 hours, stirring gently from time to time. [F]

[A] The beans can be cooked up to one day in advance. Keep covered and chilled.

[F] Freeze for up to 3 months. Defrost for 4–6 hours at room temperature or overnight in a refrigerator. Reheat for 30 minutes at 180°C, 350°F, Gas Mark 4.

Boston Baked Beans

93

POMMES DAUPHINOISES

40 g (1½ oz) butter
1 garlic clove, peeled and crushed
500 g (1¼ lb) white potatoes, peeled and thinly
sliced
salt
freshly ground black pepper
300 ml (½ pint) single cream
chopped fresh parsley, to garnish

PREPARATION TIME: 10 minutes
COOKING TIME: 1 hour 35 minutes
OVEN: 160°C, 325°F, Gas Mark 3

Clockwise from right:
Pommes Dauphinoises;
Succotash; Mixed Green
Vegetables with
Coconut Sauce

1 Butter a shallow casserole well. Melt the remaining butter in a small pan, then add the crushed garlic.

2 Layer the potatoes in the casserole, brushing each layer with the garlic butter and seasoning with salt and pepper.

3 Pour the cream over the potatoes. Cover the casserole, put into a preheated oven and cook for 1 hour. Uncover the casserole and cook for a further 30 minutes, until the potatoes are browned on top.

4 Serve garnished with fresh parsley.

SUCCOTASH

175 g (6 oz) dried lima beans, soaked overnight
2 tablespoons oil
1 onion, peeled and chopped
1 garlic clove, peeled and crushed
1 large red pepper, cored, seeded and diced
225 g (8 oz) frozen sweetcorn
salt
freshly ground black pepper

PREPARATION TIME: 10 minutes, plus
soaking
COOKING TIME: 1½ hours
OVEN: 180°C, 350°F, Gas Mark 4

This is a traditional New England dish, but as the beans came from Peru, hence the name 'Lima', that is probably where the dish originated. Lima beans are a very pale green colour in appearance and have an unusual sweet flavour. If they are not available – and they can usually be bought in health food shops – then this recipe can be made with dried butter beans. Care should be taken with the initial cooking of butter beans as they tend to fall apart if overcooked.

This makes a very good main course served with some brown rice and a green vegetable such as spinach.

1 Put the drained beans into a pan of cold water, bring to the boil, boil rapidly for 10 minutes, then reduce the heat and cook for a further 40–50 minutes until tender. [A]

2 Heat the oil in a flameproof casserole, add the onion, garlic and red pepper and cook for 2–3 minutes.

3 Drain the beans, reserving 150 ml (¼ pint) of the cooking water. Put the beans, water, sweetcorn, salt and pepper into the casserole and bring to the boil. Cover, put into a preheated oven and cook for 20 minutes. [F]

[A] The beans can be cooked up to 1 day in advance. Keep covered and chilled until required.

[F] Freeze for up to 3 months. Defrost for 4–6 hours at room temperature or overnight in a refrigerator. Reheat for 30 minutes at 180°C, 350°F, Gas Mark 4.

MIXED GREEN VEGETABLES WITH COCONUT SAUCE

100 g (4 oz) French beans, topped and tailed
225 g (8 oz) broccoli, cut into small florets
salt
175 g (6 oz) courgettes, topped and tailed and cut into thick sticks
1 green pepper, cored, seeded and cut into strips
300 ml (½ pint) plain unsweetened yogurt
150 ml (¼ pint) water
2 teaspoons cornflour
4 tablespoons desiccated coconut
2 garlic cloves, peeled
1 fresh green chilli, seeded and chopped
1 teaspoon cumin seeds
freshly ground black pepper

PREPARATION TIME: 20 minutes
COOKING TIME: 50 minutes
OVEN: 180°C, 350°F, Gas Mark 4

Cooking vegetables in a spicy coconut sauce is a typically Asian method. Originally, the milk from fresh coconuts would have been used in this dish, but desiccated coconut blended with water makes a good substitute.

This dish is very good on its own served with some Basmati rice and mango chutney or makes a very good accompaniment to other curry dishes.

1 Put the French beans and broccoli into a pan of boiling salted water and cook for 2 minutes. Add the courgettes and green pepper to the pan and cook for a further 2 minutes. Drain the vegetables well, then put into a flameproof casserole.

2 In a blender or food processor put the yogurt, water, cornflour, coconut, garlic, chilli and cumin and blend to a smooth paste. Add to the vegetables, stir well, then bring slowly to the boil, stirring all the time. Taste and adjust the seasoning, cover the casserole, put into a preheated oven and cook for about 40 minutes, until the vegetables are tender.

BROCCOLI IN WHOLEGRAIN MUSTARD SAUCE

450 g (1 lb) broccoli, cut into florets
salt
15 g (1/2 oz) butter
15 g (1/2 oz) plain flour
200 ml (7 fl oz) milk
2 teaspoons wholegrain mustard
1/2 teaspoon lemon juice
freshly ground black pepper
15 g (1/2 oz) toasted flaked almonds, to garnish

PREPARATION TIME: 10 minutes
COOKING TIME: 30–40 minutes
OVEN: 180°C, 350°F, Gas Mark 4

1 Put the broccoli into a pan of boiling salted water, bring to the boil and simmer for 3 minutes. Drain well, then put the broccoli into a casserole.

2 Melt the butter in a pan, add the flour and cook for 1 minute. Add the milk, bring to the boil and simmer for 2–3 minutes. Add the mustard, lemon juice and pepper then pour over the broccoli.

3 Cover the casserole, put into a preheated oven and cook for 20–30 minutes until the broccoli is tender.

4 Serve the casserole garnished with toasted flaked almonds.

SCALLOPED CABBAGE

750 g (1 1/2 lb) white cabbage, shredded
1 large onion, peeled and sliced
6 juniper berries, crushed
salt
75 g (3 oz) butter
25 g (1 oz) plain flour
300 ml (1/2 pint) milk
freshly ground black pepper
100 g (4 oz) fresh white breadcrumbs

PREPARATION TIME: 20 minutes
COOKING TIME: 1 hour
OVEN: 180°C, 350°F, Gas Mark 4

There are many varieties of cabbage available according to the time of year, and this recipe may be prepared using one of the other varieties or another green vegetable, such as spinach (when a garlic clove could be substituted for the juniper berries), broccoli florets or chopped Brussels sprouts.

The recipe makes a very good vegetable accompaniment. To serve as a more substantial main course add some cheese or chopped nuts to the final layer. Serve with potatoes, either baked or boiled in their skins, and carrots.

1 Put the cabbage, onion and juniper berries into a pan of boiling salted water, bring back to the boil and simmer for 5 minutes. Drain well, reserving 150 ml (1/4 pint) of the cooking water.

2 Melt 25 g (1 oz) of the butter in a pan, add the flour and cook for 1 minute. Add the milk, cabbage water and pepper, bring to the boil and cook for 3 minutes, add to the cabbage and mix well. [A]

3 Melt the remaining butter in a frying pan, add the breadcrumbs and fry until lightly browned. [A]

4 Put a third of the cabbage into a casserole and sprinkle with two tablespoons of the breadcrumbs, repeat the layers, then cover the top with the remaining breadcrumbs.

5 Put into a preheated oven and cook for 40 minutes, until the topping is golden brown.

[A] The cabbage and breadcrumbs can be prepared up to 8 hours in advance. Proceed as in the recipe.

BAKED CUCUMBER IN COTTAGE CHEESE SAUCE

25 g (1 oz) butter
1½ large cucumbers, peeled, seeded and diced
1 × 225 g (8 oz) pack cottage cheese with chives
2 tablespoons double or whipping cream
1 teaspoon chopped fresh dill or ½ teaspoon dried dillweed
salt
freshly ground black pepper

PREPARATION TIME: 10 minutes
COOKING TIME: 35 minutes
OVEN: 180°C, 350°F, Gas Mark 4

1 Melt the butter in a flameproof casserole, add the cucumber and stir around until the cucumber is coated with the butter.

2 Add the cottage cheese, cream, dill, salt and pepper, bring to the boil, cover the casserole and put into preheated oven. Cook for about 30 minutes until the cucumber is tender.

Clockwise from top:
Broccoli in Wholegrain
Mustard Sauce;
Scalloped Cabbage;
Baked Cucumber in
Cottage Cheese Sauce

97

OKRA AND PASTA CASSEROLE NIÇOISE

2 tablespoons oil
1 onion, peeled and chopped
1 garlic clove, peeled and crushed
1 × 400 g (14 oz) can chopped tomatoes
300 ml (½ pint) vegetable stock
450 g (1 lb) okra, stalk end removed and halved
1 teaspoon dried marjoram
salt
freshly ground black pepper
350 g (12 oz) pasta bows
50 g (2 oz) black olives

PREPARATION TIME: 15 minutes
COOKING TIME: 1 hour
OVEN: 180°C, 350°F, Gas Mark 4

1 Heat the oil in a flameproof casserole, add the onion and garlic and cook for 2–3 minutes, add the tomatoes and their juice, stock, okra, marjoram, salt and pepper and bring to the boil. Cover the casserole, put into a preheated oven and cook for 40 minutes.

2 While the okra is cooking, put the pasta into a pan of boiling salted water and cook for 5 minutes. Drain well and rinse with cold water.

3 After the casserole has been in the oven for 40 minutes, add the pasta and olives, mix well, cover the casserole again and cook for a further 15 minutes.

MIXED BEAN CASSEROLE WITH CASHEW CRUMBLE

225 g (8 oz) shelled weight broad beans
225 g (8 oz) runner beans, sliced
100 g (4 oz) French beans, topped and tailed
25 g (1 oz) butter
25 g (1 oz) plain flour
300 ml (½ pint) milk
2 tablespoons chopped fresh parsley
salt
freshly ground black pepper

TOPPING:
75 g (3 oz) butter
100 g (4 oz) plain flour
50 g (2 oz) rolled oats
50 g (2 oz) salted cashew nuts, chopped

PREPARATION TIME: 25 minutes
COOKING TIME: 55 minutes
OVEN: 200°C, 400°F, Gas Mark 6

This is a very useful basic recipe as many variations can be based on it, both with the filling and the topping. It is a good way of using up small quantities both of fresh vegetables and of leftover cooked vegetables. The sauce can be varied to suit the vegetables, using, for instance, cheese or tomato flavours.

Cashew nuts are very high in protein but, if they are not available, any other chopped nuts may be used. Breadcrumbs and wheatgerm can be used instead of the rolled oats or, if nuts are not used, some grated cheese can be added to the crumble for extra protein.

1 Put the broad beans into a pan of boiling salted water, cook for 5 minutes, then add the runner beans and French beans and cook for a further 5 minutes. Drain the beans well, then put into a shallow casserole.

2 Melt the butter in a pan, add the flour and cook for 2 minutes. Add the milk, bring to the boil, stirring all the time, then simmer for 2–3 minutes. Add the parsley, salt and pepper, pour over the beans and mix well. [A]

3 Rub the butter and flour together, then add the rolled oats and cashew nuts. [A]

4 Sprinkle the topping over the beans, pressing it down lightly. Put the casserole into a preheated oven and cook for 40 minutes.

[A] The vegetables and crumble topping can be prepared up to 8 hours in advance, then proceed with the recipe.

ITALIAN BEAN CASSEROLE

100 g (4 oz) red kidney beans, soaked overnight
100 g (4 oz) cannellini beans, soaked overnight
100 g (4 oz) flageolet beans, soaked overnight
2 tablespoons olive oil
1 onion, peeled and chopped
1 green pepper, cored, seeded and chopped
1 teaspoon dried oregano
1 × 150 g (5 oz) can tomato purée
300 ml (½ pint) water
1 teaspoon caster sugar
salt
freshly ground black pepper
sprig of fresh oregano, to garnish

PREPARATION TIME: 15 minutes, plus
soaking
COOKING TIME: 1¾ hours
OVEN: 160°C, 325°F, Gas Mark 3

1 Cook the beans separately, to avoid the red
beans colouring the others. Cover with cold
water, bring to the boil, boil rapidly for 10
minutes, then reduce the heat and cook until the
beans are just cooked. [A]

2 Heat the oil in a pan, add the onion and green
pepper and cook until soft.

3 Add the oregano, tomato purée, water,
sugar, salt and pepper to the pan and bring to
the boil.

4 Drain the beans, put into a casserole, pour
the onion and pepper sauce over them, then put
into a preheated oven uncovered and cook for
1 hour, stirring frequently but gently until
most of the liquid has been absorbed. [F]

5 Serve the casserole garnished with fresh
oregano.

[A] The beans can be cooked up to 1 day in
advance. Keep covered and chilled.

[F] Freeze for up to 3 months. Defrost for 4–6
hours at room temperature or overnight in a
refrigerator. Reheat for 30 minutes at 180°C,
350°F, Gas Mark 4.

From the top: Okra and Pasta Casserole Niçoise;
Mixed Bean Casserole with Cashew Crumble;
Italian Bean Casserole

CHINESE CABBAGE WITH TOMATO AND GINGER

1 head of Chinese cabbage, approx. 750 g-1 kg
(1½-2 lbs)
2 tablespoons oil
1 large onion, peeled and sliced
2 tablespoons tomato purée
200 ml (7 fl oz) water
1 teaspoon caster sugar
2 teaspoons grated root ginger
salt
freshly ground black pepper

PREPARATION TIME: 10 minutes
COOKING TIME: 30 minutes
OVEN: 180°C, 350°F, Gas Mark 4

Clockwise from top:
Baked Lemon Carrots;
Chinese Cabbage with
Tomato and Ginger;
Sauerkraut with Orange
and Raisins

If Chinese cabbage is not available, this dish can be made with celery. Either cut the celery into thick chunks or use celery hearts which are often available in packs. If celery hearts are used the cooking time should be increased to 40–45 minutes.

1 Cut the Chinese cabbage into thick slices, removing and discarding the core.

2 Heat the oil in a flameproof casserole, add the onion and cabbage and stir around until the vegetables are coated with the oil.

3 Add the tomato purée, water, sugar, ginger, salt and pepper and bring to the boil.

4 Cover the casserole, put into a preheated oven and cook for 25 minutes.

BAKED LEMON CARROTS

25 g (1 oz) butter
1 tablespoon soft brown sugar
1 tablespoon lemon juice
500 g (1¼ lb) carrots, peeled and cut into even-sized
pieces
300 ml (¼ pint) water
salt
freshly ground black pepper
2 teaspoons grated lemon rind, to garnish

PREPARATION TIME: 10 minutes
COOKING TIME: 30–35 minutes
OVEN: 180°C, 350°F, Gas Mark 4

Parsnips are very good cooked by this method. Cut the parsnips into large even-sized pieces and remove the core. As parsnips have a natural sweetness of their own, 1-2 teaspoons of sugar should be sufficient.

1 Melt the butter in a flameproof casserole, add the brown sugar and lemon juice, then add the carrots and stir them into the sugar and juice until they are well coated.

2 Pour in the water, add the salt and pepper and bring to the boil. Cover the casserole and transfer to a preheated oven. Cook for 20–25 minutes, until the carrots are just cooked.

3 Remove the casserole from the oven, put back on the heat, and bring to the boil, stirring gently until the liquid has evaporated and the carrots are coated with a buttery glaze. Serve sprinkled with the lemon rind.

SAUERKRAUT WITH ORANGE AND RAISINS

500 g (1¼ lb) sauerkraut
1 onion, peeled and sliced
grated rind and juice of 1 orange
50 g (2 oz) raisins
pepper
150 ml (¼ pint) water
1 orange, segmented
25 g (1 oz) melted butter

PREPARATION TIME: 15 minutes
COOKING TIME: 1 hour 10 minutes
OVEN: 180°C, 350°F, Gas Mark 4

Sauerkraut is a German method of preserving white cabbage by shredding and salting it and allowing it to ferment. It is sold loose in delicatessens and on delicatessen counters in supermarkets and is also available in cans and jars.

For a delicious variation on this recipe substitute 425 g (15 oz) can of pineapple chunks in syrup for the orange and raisins. Use the syrup from the can instead of the orange juice, then stir the pineapple chunks into the casserole for the last 15 minutes of cooking time.

1 Mix together the sauerkraut, onion, orange rind and juice, raisins, pepper and water in a casserole.

2 Cover the casserole and put into a preheated oven. Cook for 1 hour, stirring from time to time and adding a little extra water if it appears to be drying out.

3 Remove the casserole from the oven and uncover. Put the orange segments on top of the sauerkraut and brush with the melted butter. Return to the oven uncovered and cook for a further 10 minutes.

SAG DHAL

2 tablespoons oil
1 onion, peeled and chopped
1 garlic clove, peeled and crushed
1 teaspoon grated fresh ginger
½ teaspoon ground turmeric
1 teaspoon ground cumin
1 teaspoon mustard seeds
½ teaspoon cayenne pepper
175 g (6 oz) whole green lentils, soaked overnight
600 ml (1 pint) water
450 g (1 lb) spinach, washed and shredded, or 225 g
(8 oz) frozen leaf spinach, thawed
salt
150 ml (5 fl oz) plain unsweetened yogurt

PREPARATION TIME: 15 minutes, plus
soaking
COOKING TIME: 1 hour 10 minutes
OVEN: 160°C, 325°F, Gas Mark 3

1 Heat the oil in a flameproof casserole, add the
onion, garlic and ginger and cook for 2
minutes, then add the turmeric, cumin, mustard seeds and cayenne and cook for a further
minute.

2 Add the drained lentils to the casserole, add
the water and bring to the boil, then add the
spinach and salt.

3 Cover the casserole, put into a preheated
oven and cook for 1 hour, stirring gently from
time to time. [F]

4 Spoon the yogurt over the casserole before
serving.

[F] Freeze for up to 3 months. Defrost overnight in the refrigerator or for 4–6 hours at
room temperature. Reheat at 180°C, 350°F, Gas
Mark 4 for 20–25 minutes.

From the top: Sag Dhal; Vegetable Dhansak;
Mushroom and Millet Casserole with Coriander

VEGETABLE DHANSAK

100 g (4 oz) red lentils
2 tablespoons oil
1 onion, peeled and chopped
1 garlic clove, peeled and crushed
1 teaspoon ground cumin
1/2 teaspoon ground coriander
1 teaspoon cardamom seeds
pinch ground cinnamon
2 teaspoons white wine vinegar
1 tablespoon mild lime pickle
450 ml (3/4 pint) water
225 g (8 oz) aubergine, stalk removed and diced
225 g (8 oz) sweet potato, peeled and diced
225 g (8 oz) potato, peeled and diced
salt
freshly ground black pepper
sprig of fresh coriander, to garnish

PREPARATION TIME: 20 minutes
COOKING TIME: 1¼ hours
OVEN: 180°C, 350°F, Gas Mark 4

1 Put the lentils into a pan of cold water, bring to the boil and simmer for 10 minutes. Drain well. [A]

2 Heat the oil in a pan, add the onion and garlic and cook until soft. Add the spices to the pan, cook for 1 minute, then add the vinegar, pickle and water and bring to the boil.

3 Put the lentils into a casserole, add the contents of the pan, season with salt and pepper and mix well.

4 Cover the casserole, put into preheated oven and cook for 1 hour, stirring gently from time to time. [F]

5 Serve garnished with fresh coriander.

[A] The lentils can be cooked up to 1 day in advance. Keep covered and chilled.

[F] Freeze for up to 3 months, defrost overnight in a refrigerator or 4–6 hours at room temperature. Reheat at 180°C, 350°F, Gas Mark 4 for 20–30 minutes.

MUSHROOM AND MILLET CASSEROLE WITH CORIANDER

225 g (8 oz) millet
salt
50 g (2 oz) butter
1 onion, peeled and chopped
2 garlic cloves, peeled and crushed
450 g (1 lb) flat mushrooms, peeled and diced
2 teaspoons soy sauce
85 ml (3 fl oz) water
1 teaspoon ground coriander
2 tablespoons chopped fresh coriander
freshly ground black pepper
3-4 tomatoes, skinned and sliced

PREPARATION TIME: 15 minutes
COOKING TIME: 1¼ hours
OVEN: 180°C, 350°F, Gas Mark 4

1 Put the millet into a pan of lightly salted water, bring to the boil and simmer for about 30 minutes until tender. [A]

2 Melt the butter in a pan, add the onion and garlic and cook for 2 minutes, then add the mushrooms and cook for a further 3 minutes, turning the mushrooms in the butter.

3 Drain the millet, combine the millet and mushroom mixture in a casserole, then add the soy sauce, water, ground and fresh coriander. Stir well, taste and adjust the seasoning, if necessary.

4 Cover the casserole, put into a preheated oven and cook for 30 minutes. Remove the casserole from the oven, uncover and put the sliced tomatoes on top of the millet. Return to the oven uncovered and cook for a further 10 minutes.

[A] The millet can be cooked up to 1 day in advance. Keep covered and chilled.

WINTER VEGETABLE HOT POT

2 tablespoons oil
1 large onion, peeled and chopped
1 large leek, washed and sliced
225 g (8 oz) carrots, peeled and diced
225 g (8 oz) swede, peeled and diced
100 g (4 oz) parsnips, peeled and diced
50 g (2 oz) pearl barley
600 ml (1 pint) vegetable stock
salt
freshly ground black pepper
450 g (1 lb) potatoes, peeled and thinly sliced
15 g (½ oz) melted butter

PREPARATION TIME: 20 minutes
COOKING TIME: 1 hour 50 minutes–
2 hours
OVEN: 190°C, 375°F, Gas Mark 5; then:
220°C, 425°F, Gas Mark 7

Clockwise from top left:
Winter Vegetable Hot
Pot; Baked Colcannon;
Brussels Sprouts and
Mushroom Casserole
with Cheese Batter
Topping

1 Heat the oil in a pan, add the onion and leek and cook until soft. Put the carrots, swede and parsnips into the pan, add the pearl barley, 450 ml (¾ pint) of the stock, salt and pepper. Bring to the boil then transfer the contents of the pan to a casserole.

2 Layer the potatoes over the vegetables in the casserole. Pour over the remaining stock and brush the potatoes with the melted butter. Cover the casserole, put into a preheated oven and cook for 1½ hours.

3 Uncover the casserole, increase the heat and cook for a further 15 minutes to brown the potatoes.

BAKED COLCANNON

450 g (1 lb) potatoes, peeled
salt
225 g (8 oz) curly kale
50 g (8 oz) butter
1 bunch spring onions, chopped
2 tablespoons single cream or top of the milk
freshly ground black pepper
50 g (2 oz) grated Cheddar cheese

PREPARATION TIME: 15 minutes
COOKING TIME: 45 minutes
OVEN: 200°C, 400°F, Gas Mark 6

1 Put the potatoes into a pan of salted water, bring to the boil, cover and simmer for 10 minutes. Add the kale to the pan and cook for a further 10 minutes. Drain well. [A]

2 Use a little of the butter to grease a shallow casserole. Melt the remaining butter in a pan, add the spring onions and cook for 2–3 minutes. Add the potatoes and kale, cream and pepper and mash well.

3 Transfer the mixture to the casserole, sprinkle with the grated cheese, put uncovered into a preheated oven and cook for 20 minutes.

[A] The potatoes and kale can be prepared up to 1 day in advance. Keep covered and chilled.

BRUSSELS SPROUTS AND MUSHROOM CASSEROLE WITH CHEESE BATTER TOPPING

450 g (1 lb) trimmed weight Brussels sprouts
salt
25 g (1 oz) butter
1 onion, peeled and chopped
225 g (8 oz) button mushrooms, wiped
15 g (½ oz) plain flour
freshly ground black pepper

FOR THE TOPPING:
100 g (4 oz) self-raising flour
2 eggs, beaten
150 ml (¼ pint) milk
75 g (3 oz) strong Cheddar cheese, grated

PREPARATION TIME: 25 minutes
COOKING TIME: 50 minutes
OVEN: 200°C, 400°F, Gas Mark 6

1 Put the Brussels sprouts into a pan of boiling salted water, cook for 5 minutes then drain, reserving 150 ml (¼ pint) of the cooking liquid. Put the Brussels sprouts into a shallow casserole.

2 Melt the butter in a pan, add the onion and cook until soft, then add the mushrooms and cook for a further minute.

3 Add the plain flour to the pan, cook for 1 minute, then add the reserved liquid. Bring to the boil, taste and adjust the seasoning, if necessary, and pour over the Brussels sprouts, mixing well. [A]

4 For the topping, sift the self-raising flour into a bowl, add the eggs, milk and all but 1 tablespoon of the cheese. Add a little salt and pepper then pour over the vegetables in the casserole. Sprinkle with the remaining cheese.

5 Put the casserole, uncovered, into a pre-heated oven and cook for 40 minutes.

[A] The vegetables can be prepared up to 8 hours in advance. Cover and keep cool until required.

SPANISH GREEN BEAN CASSEROLE

350 g (12 oz) French beans, topped and tailed
salt
25 g (1 oz) butter
1 small onion, peeled and finely chopped
1 small green pepper, cored, seeded and finely chopped
15 g (½ oz) plain flour
175 ml (6 fl oz) tomato juice
freshly ground black pepper
50 g (2 oz) brown breadcrumbs
25 g (1 oz) grated Cheddar cheese

PREPARATION TIME: 15 minutes
COOKING TIME: 35 minutes
OVEN: 180°C, 350°F, Gas Mark 4

1 Put the beans into a pan of boiling salted water and cook for 5 minutes. Drain well then put into a shallow casserole.

2 Melt the butter in a pan, add the onion and pepper and cook until soft. Stir in the flour and cook for 1 minute, then add the tomato juice and pepper and bring to the boil. Pour the sauce over the beans in the casserole and mix well.

3 Mix together the breadcrumbs and cheese and spread in an even layer over the beans. Put the uncovered casserole into a preheated oven and cook for 25 minutes.

CREAMED LEEK AND JERUSALEM ARTICHOKE CASSEROLE

450 g (1 lb) Jerusalem artichokes, peeled and cut into bite-size pieces
1 teaspoon lemon juice
salt
25 g (1 oz) butter
450 g (1 lb) leeks, washed and sliced
1 tablespoon plain flour
150 ml (5 fl oz) single cream
50 g (2 oz) flaked almonds
1 teaspoon coriander seeds
freshly ground black pepper

PREPARATION TIME: 15 minutes
COOKING TIME: 45–50 minutes
OVEN: 180°C, 350°F, Gas Mark 4

1 Put the artichokes into a pan of cold water with the lemon juice and a little salt.

2 Bring to the boil, reduce the heat and simmer for 2 minutes. Drain, reserving 150 ml (¼ pint) of the water.

3 Melt the butter in a pan, add the leeks and cook for 2–3 minutes.

4 Add the flour to the pan, cook for 1 minute, then add the artichoke water and cream. Add the artichokes, almonds and coriander seeds. Taste and adjust the seasoning, if necessary.

5 Transfer the mixture to a casserole, cover and cook for 30–35 minutes, until the vegetables are tender.

PEPPERONATA

225 g (8 oz) green peppers, cored and seeded
225 g (8 oz) red peppers, cored and seeded
225 g (8 oz) yellow peppers, cored and seeded
2 tablespoons olive oil
1 large onion (Spanish, for preference), peeled and sliced
350 g (12 oz) tomatoes, skinned, seeded and chopped
salt
freshly ground black pepper

PREPARATION TIME: 15 minutes
COOKING TIME: 30–40 minutes
OVEN: 180°C, 350°F, Gas Mark 4

1 Cut the peppers into even-sized pieces. Heat the oil in a flameproof casserole, add the onion and cook until soft.

2 Add the peppers, tomatoes, salt and pepper to the casserole and cook until the tomatoes becomes a thick purée.

3 Cover the casserole, put into a preheated oven and cook for 20–30 minutes, until the peppers are soft.

Clockwise from top:
Spanish Green Bean
Casserole; Pepperonata;
Creamed Leek and
Jerusalem Artichoke
Casserole

EXOTIC

FLAVOURS

Traditional flavours from round the world are
used in the deliciously aromatic recipes in this
chapter. There is a Moroccan stew, or tagine, in
which lamb is spiced with ginger, cinnamon and
prunes and a piquant version of the Mexican
Chilli con Carne. From northern Europe comes
Danish Dilled Lamb and Asparagus Casserole
and from the Middle East Armenian Lamb, in
which apricots, coriander, cumin and cinnamon
turn lamb into a truly exotic dish. Among the
flavourings in the casseroles, some, like star
anise and pomegranates, may come as delicious
surprises to a British palate, while others, familiar
enough in themselves, are combined unexpectedly:
Mackerel with Sesame and Orange, for
instance, or Turkey Mole with chocolate.

DANISH DILLED LAMB AND ASPARAGUS CASSEROLE

*750 g (1½ lb) boned weight loin of lamb, rolled and
tied
900 ml (1½ pints) hot lamb stock
salt
freshly ground black pepper
1 teaspoon dillweed
450 g (1 lb) asparagus
15 g (½ oz) butter
15 g (½ oz) plain flour
150 ml (5 fl oz) soured cream
fresh dill sprigs, to garnish*

PREPARATION TIME: 15 minutes
COOKING TIME: 1¾ hours
OVEN: 160°C, 325°F, Gas Mark 3

1 Put the lamb into a casserole, add the stock,
salt, pepper and dill weed, cover the casserole,
place it in a preheated oven and cook for 1½
hours.

2 Pour off about 1 pint of the stock from the
casserole and cook the asparagus in this stock
on top of the stove for 5–10 minutes until
tender.

3 Take the lamb out of the casserole, remove
the string and keep warm. Pour the remaining
stock into a saucepan, skimming off any fat
from the top, and boil down until reduced to
about 200 ml (7 fl oz).

4 Mix the butter and flour together, take the
saucepan off the heat and whisk the butter
mixture into the hot stock. Bring the stock to
the boil and cook for 2–3 minutes. Stir in the
soured cream and reheat, but do not boil.

5 Slice the lamb and arrange it on a warmed
serving dish. Top with the asparagus and pour
the sauce over. Garnish with the sprigs of fresh
dill.

TAGINE

*2 tablespoons oil
500 g (1¼ lb) lean lamb, diced
1 large onion, peeled and chopped
1 garlic clove, peeled and crushed
1 teaspoon ground ginger
1 teaspoon ground cinnamon
25 g (1 oz) plain flour
300 ml (½ pint) lamb stock
salt
freshly ground black pepper
225 g (8 oz) pitted prunes, soaked overnight and
drained
1 tablespoon toasted sesame seeds, to garnish*

PREPARATION TIME: 15 minutes, plus
soaking
COOKING TIME: 1 hour 40 minutes
OVEN: 180°C, 350°F, Gas Mark 4

This traditional Moroccan stew is cooked in a
tagine, a round and shallow earthenware pot
with a conical lid. These tagines can sometimes
be bought in kitchenware shops in this country.

1 Heat the oil in a frying pan, add the meat and
cook until it is brown on all sides. Remove the
meat from the pan with a slotted spoon and put
into a casserole.

2 Fry the onion and garlic in the pan until soft,
then add the spices and cook for 1 minute.

3 Sprinkle the flour into the pan and cook for 1
minute, then add the stock, salt and pepper.
Bring to the boil, then pour over the lamb.
Cover the casserole, place in a preheated oven
and cook for 1 hour.

4 Add the prunes to the casserole and cook for
a further 30 minutes. [F]

5 Transfer the lamb and prunes to a warmed
serving dish and sprinkle with the sesame seeds
before serving.

[F] Freeze for up to 3 months, defrost overnight
in the refrigerator or for 4–6 hours at room
temperature. Reheat at 180°C, 350°F, Gas Mark
4 for 30–40 minutes, then proceed as in the
recipe.

KIBBEH IN MINT AND YOGURT SAUCE

350 g (12 oz) finely minced lamb
100 g (4 oz) bulghar, soaked for 30 minutes
1 onion, peeled and grated
salt
freshly ground black pepper
1 teaspoon ground allspice
1 teaspoon ground nutmeg
oil for frying
1 garlic clove, peeled and crushed
300 ml (½ pint) lamb stock
2 teaspoons cornflour
200 ml (7 fl oz) plain Greek-style yogurt
1 tablespoon chopped fresh mint
mint leaves, to garnish

PREPARATION TIME: 20 minutes, plus
soaking and chilling
COOKING TIME: 1 hour 10 minutes
OVEN: 180°C, 350°F, Gas Mark 4

1 Put the lamb, bulghar, onion, salt, pepper, allspice and nutmeg into a bowl and mix well. Divide the mixture into 8 and form into oval shapes. Chill for 30 minutes.

2 Heat the oil in a frying pan and fry the kibbeh until they are brown all over, then transfer them to a casserole.

3 Drain off most of the oil from the pan, add the garlic and cook for 1–2 minutes. Add the stock, bring to the boil, then pour over the kibbeh. Cover the casserole, put it into a preheated oven and cook for 1 hour.

4 Remove the casserole from the oven, pour the stock into a saucepan and keep the kibbeh warm. Mix together the cornflour and yogurt and whisk into the stock. Bring slowly to the boil. Add the chopped mint and pour the sauce over the kibbeh in the casserole. Garnish the dish with the mint leaves before serving.

Clockwise from top:
Danish Dilled Lamb and
Asparagus Casserole;
Tagine; Kibbeh in Mint
and Yogurt Sauce

GREEK LAMB AND FETTA CHEESE CASSEROLE

750 g (1½ lb) boned weight leg of lamb, bone removed
3 tablespoons olive oil
1 large onion, peeled and finely chopped
1 garlic clove, peeled and crushed
1 × 400 g (14 oz) can tomatoes, drained and chopped
1 teaspoon dried oregano
100 g (4 oz) black olives, stoned and chopped
salt
freshly ground black pepper
225 g (8 oz) fetta cheese
black olives, to garnish

PREPARATION TIME: 20 minutes
COOKING TIME: 1¾ hours
OVEN: 160°C, 325°F, Gas Mark 3

1 Cut the leg of lamb into thin slices. Heat the oil in a frying pan and fry the lamb slices a few at a time. Drain on paper towels.

2 Add the onion and garlic to the pan and cook for 2–3 minutes, then add the tomatoes, oregano, olives, salt and pepper.

3 Layer the meat and tomato mixture in a casserole, finishing with a layer of the tomato mixture. Crumble the fetta cheese over the top. Cover the casserole, put into a preheated oven and cook for 1½ hours.

4 Remove the casserole from the oven, uncover and place under a preheated hot grill to brown the cheese.

5 Serve garnished with black olives.

From the top: Greek Lamb and Fetta Cheese Casserole; Armenian Lamb; Dolmades

ARMENIAN LAMB

SERVES 4-6
2 tablespoons olive oil
1 kg (2 lb) boned weight leg of lamb, tied
1 onion, peeled and chopped
175 g (6 oz) dried apricots
1 teaspoon ground coriander
1 teaspoon ground cumin
1 teaspoon ground cinnamon
salt
freshly ground black pepper
about 900 ml (1½ pints) lamb stock
25 g (1 oz) toasted pine nuts, to garnish

PREPARATION TIME: 15 minutes
COOKING TIME: 2 hours 10 minutes
OVEN: 160°C, 325°F, Gas Mark 3

1 Heat the oil in a flameproof casserole, brown the lamb on all sides, then add the onion to the pan and cook until it has softened slightly.

2 Add the apricots, spices, salt and pepper to the pan with enough stock to come half way up the lamb. Bring to the boil, cover the casserole and transfer to a preheated oven. Cook for 2 hours, turning the lamb from time to time.

3 Remove the casserole from the oven. Remove the strings from the lamb and keep it warm in a deep serving dish.

4 Put the onions and apricots into a blender or food processor with enough stock from the casserole (fat skimmed off) to make 600 ml (1 pint). Blend into a smooth sauce. Reheat if necessary, pour over the lamb and serve sprinkled with the pine nuts.

DOLMADES

1 tablespoon olive oil
1 onion, peeled and finely chopped
350 g (12 oz) minced lamb
2 tablespoons tomato purée
450 ml (¾ pint) water
salt
freshly ground black pepper
175 g (6 oz) cooked long-grain rice
2 tablespoons chopped fresh parsley
1 × 225 g (8 oz) packet vine leaves
2 teaspoons lemon juice
½ teaspoon caster sugar

PREPARATION TIME: 25 minutes
COOKING TIME: 1 hour 10 minutes
OVEN: 180°C, 350°F, Gas Mark 4

1 Heat the oil in a pan, add the onion and lamb and cook until the lamb is no longer pink. Add 1 tablespoon of the tomato purée, 150 ml (¼ pint) of the water, salt and pepper. Bring to the boil, cover the pan and cook for 20 minutes.

2 Remove the pan from the heat, add the rice and parsley to the pan and mix well. [A]

3 Put the vine leaves into a pan of boiling water and cook for 5 minutes. Drain well.

4 Put two teaspoons of the lamb mixture into the centre of each vine leaf, using two leaves together if they are small, and fold the leaves up to make small packets. There should be about 24 packets in all.

5 Put the packets in a single layer, seam side down, in a shallow casserole. Mix together the remaining tomato purée and water, the lemon juice and sugar and pour over the vine leaves.

6 Cover the casserole and put into a preheated oven and cook for 40 minutes.

[A] The filling can be prepared up to 1 day in advance. Keep covered and chilled.

MUGHLAI CHICKEN

1 × 1½ kg (3 lb) chicken
25 g (1 oz) butter
1 tablespoon oil
450 g (1 lb) onions, peeled and chopped
1 clove garlic, peeled and crushed
1 teaspoon ground coriander
½ teaspoon ground ginger
pinch ground cloves
1 teaspoon ground chilli powder
1 teaspoon cardamom seeds
2 teaspoons ground cumin
1 teaspoon ground turmeric
150 ml (5 fl oz) double or whipping cream
150 ml (5 fl oz) plain unsweetened yogurt
salt
freshly ground black pepper

TO GARNISH:
sprigs of fresh coriander
raw onion rings

Clockwise from top:
Mughlai Chicken;
Mexican Chicken in
Green Almond Sauce;
Circassian Chicken

PREPARATION TIME: 20 minutes
COOKING TIME: 1 hour 40 minutes
OVEN: 190°C, 375°F, Gas Mark 5

1 Skin the chicken and put into a casserole.

2 Melt the butter and oil together in a pan, add the onions and garlic and cook until softened. Mix the spices together, add to the pan and cook for 1–2 minutes.

3 Put the cream and yogurt into a blender or food processor, add the onion and spice mixture, salt and pepper, and blend to a smooth purée.

4 Pour over the chicken, cover the casserole, put into a preheated oven and cook for 1½ hours, basting the chicken from time to time.

5 Remove the casserole from the oven, transfer the chicken to a heated serving dish and pour the sauce over. Garnish with fresh coriander and rings of raw onion.

MEXICAN CHICKEN IN GREEN ALMOND SAUCE

4 chicken joints, approx. 350 g (12 oz) each
1 onion, peeled and chopped
1 clove garlic, peeled and crushed
1 green chilli, seeds removed
salt
freshly ground black pepper
300 ml (½ pint) hot chicken stock
large bunch parsley, stalks removed
large bunch fresh coriander, stalks removed
50 g (2 oz) ground almonds
25 g (1 oz) flaked almonds

PREPARATION TIME: 15 minutes
COOKING TIME: 1¼–1½ hours
OVEN: 180°C, 350°F, Gas Mark 4

1 Skin the chicken joints and put them in an even layer in a casserole, add the onion, garlic, green chilli, salt and pepper and pour the stock over. Cover the casserole and cook in a preheated oven for 1–1¼ hours until the chicken is cooked.

2 Remove the casserole from the oven, put the stock, onion, garlic and green chilli into a blender or food processor, then add the parsley, fresh coriander and ground almonds. Blend to a thick sauce. Taste and adjust the seasoning, if necessary.

3 Sprinkle the flaked almonds over the chicken and pour the sauce over. [F] Recover the casserole and return to the oven for a further 15 minutes to heat through.

4 Serve the casserole with a watercress and cherry tomato salad, if liked.

[F] Freeze for up to 3 months. Defrost overnight in the refrigerator or for 4–6 hours at room temperature. Reheat at 180°C, 350°F, Gas Mark 4 for about 40 minutes.

CIRCASSIAN CHICKEN

1 × 1½ kg (3 lb) chicken, jointed
1 onion, peeled and chopped
1 carrot, peeled and chopped
1 celery stick, chopped
3 parsley stalks
salt
freshly ground black pepper
2 slices white bread, crusts removed
225 g (8 oz) shelled walnuts
2 tablespoons oil (walnut if possible)
2 teaspoons paprika

TO GARNISH:
sprigs of fresh chervil
walnut pieces

PREPARATION TIME: 15 minutes, plus cooling
COOKING TIME: 1–1¼ hours
OVEN: 180°C, 350°F, Gas Mark 4

1 Put the chicken into a casserole with the onion, carrot, celery, parsley stalks, salt and pepper. Cover with boiling water, put into a preheated oven and cook for 1–1¼ hours until the chicken is cooked.

2 Remove the casserole from the oven and leave it until the chicken is cool enough to handle. Strain the stock and reserve, discarding the vegetables.

3 Skin and bone the chicken, then cut into small pieces. Place on a serving dish. [A]

4 Put the bread, walnuts and 300 ml (½ pint) of the reserved stock into a blender or food processor and blend into a thick sauce. Taste and adjust the seasoning, if necessary, and pour over the chicken.

5 Mix together the oil and paprika and sprinkle over the chicken and sauce. Garnish with fresh chervil and walnut pieces and serve at room temperature.

[A] The chicken can be cooked up to one day in advance and kept covered and chilled until needed. Proceed as above.

NIGERIAN CHICKEN AND PEANUT CASSEROLE

2 tablespoons oil
1 large onion, peeled and chopped
½ teaspoon chilli powder
1 teaspoon ground cumin
300 ml (½ pint) chicken stock
100 g (4 oz) crunchy peanut butter
salt
freshly ground black pepper
4 chicken joints, approx 350 g (12 oz) each
225 g (8 oz) tomatoes, peeled, seeded and chopped

TO GARNISH:
chilli powder
finely chopped fresh parsley

PREPARATION TIME: 15 minutes
COOKING TIME: 1 hour 20 minutes
OVEN: 180°C, 350°F, Gas Mark 4

This recipe is best made with a standard peanut butter containing an emulsifier. If a peanut butter without an emulsifier is used, 1 teaspoon of cornflour should be added to the stock with the peanut butter to prevent the oil in it separating.

1 Heat the oil in a pan, add the onion and fry until it is soft. Add the chilli and cumin to the pan and cook for 1 minute. Add the stock, peanut butter, salt and pepper and bring to the boil, stirring well.

2 Skin the chicken joints and put into a casserole, add the tomatoes and cover with the peanut sauce.

3 Cover the casserole, put into a preheated oven and cook for 1-1¼ hours until the chicken is very tender, turning the chicken from time to time. [F]

4 Garnish with a little chilli powder and the finely chopped fresh parsley.

[F] Freeze for up to 3 months. Defrost overnight in the refrigerator or for 4–6 hours at room temperature. Reheat at 180°C, 350°F, Gas Mark 4 for about 40 minutes.

POLYNESIAN POUSSIN

3 tablespoons oil
4 × 450 g (1 lb) poussins
1 × 450 g (1 lb) can pineapple chunks in syrup
chicken stock
2 teaspoons cornflour
1 tablespoon tomato purée
1 onion, peeled and sliced
1 red pepper, cored, seeded and sliced
salt
freshly ground black pepper
50 g (2 oz) macadamia nuts, chopped

PREPARATION TIME: 15 minutes
COOKING TIME: 1 hour 10 minutes–1 hour 25 minutes
OVEN: 190°C, 375°F, Gas Mark 5

1 Heat the oil in a frying pan and brown the poussins on all sides, then transfer them to a casserole, reserving the oil in the frying pan.

2 Drain the syrup from the pineapple and make up to 300 ml (½ pint) with chicken stock. Mix a little of this liquid with the cornflour and tomato purée, put all the liquid into a small saucepan, bring to the boil and pour over the poussins.

3 Cover the casserole, put into a preheated oven and cook for 1-1¼ hours until the poussins are tender, basting them occasionally.

4 When the poussins are cooked, heat the reserved oil in the frying pan and lightly fry the onion and pepper until soft.

5 Strain the liquid from the casserole into the frying pan, add the pineapple and salt and pepper and boil up until the mixture becomes syrupy.

6 Put the poussins on to a warmed serving dish, pour the sauce over and sprinkle with the macadamia nuts.

MOROCCAN CHICKEN WITH SAFFRON, LEMON AND OLIVES

4 boned chicken breasts with skin retained, approx
175 g (6 oz) each
2 tablespoons clear honey
15 g (½ oz) butter
85 ml (3 fl oz) chicken stock
pinch saffron
½ teaspoon ground ginger
½ teaspoon ground turmeric
2 tablespoons lemon juice
salt
freshly ground black pepper
100 g (4 oz) green olives, stoned

TO GARNISH:
4 lemon wedges
fresh chives

PREPARATION TIME: 10 minutes
COOKING TIME: 50 minutes
OVEN: 200°C, 400°F, Gas Mark 6

1 Brush the chicken skin with a little of the honey. Melt the butter in a frying pan, put the chicken in, skin side down, and cook gently until the skin is a rich brown colour, taking care not to burn it.

2 Put the chicken, skin side up, into a shallow casserole. Pour the stock, remaining honey, saffron, ginger, turmeric, lemon juice and salt and pepper into the pan, bring to the boil and pour around the chicken breasts in the casserole. The liquid should not cover the skin.

3 Put into a preheated oven and cook, uncovered, for 40 minutes. Add the olives to the casserole and cook for a further 5 minutes.

4 Serve garnished with the lemon wedges and chives.

From the top: Nigerian Chicken and Peanut Casserole; Polynesian Poussin; Moroccan Chicken with Saffron, Lemon and Olives

CHINESE FIVE-SPICE CHICKEN LEGS

1 tablespoon sesame oil
8 chicken drumsticks, skinned
1 small bunch spring onions, sliced
1 × 225 g (8 oz) can bamboo shoots, drained
2 teaspoons cornflour
2 tablespoons soy sauce
3 tablespoons dry sherry
85 ml (3 fl oz) water
2 teaspoons five-spice powder
salt
freshly ground black pepper

PREPARATION TIME: 10 minutes
COOKING TIME: 1 hour 10 minutes
OVEN: 180°C, 350°F, Gas Mark 4

Clockwise from top:
Chinese Five-Spice
Chicken Legs; Chilli con
Carne; Madagascan
Carpetbag Steak

Five-spice powder is available from some supermarkets and from Chinese delicatessens.

1 Heat the oil in a pan and lightly fry the chicken drumsticks in it. Transfer them to a casserole, then add the spring onions, reserving 1 tablespoonful for garnish, and the bamboo shoots.

2 Mix the cornflour with the soy sauce, sherry, water and five-spice powder, add to the oil remaining in the pan, bring to the boil, taste and adjust the seasoning, then pour over the chicken drumsticks.

3 Cover the casserole, then put into a preheated oven and cook for 1 hour.

4 Serve garnished with the reserved spring onions.

MADAGASCAN CARPETBAG STEAK

1 large slice buttock steak, approx 750 g (1½ lb)
25 g (1 oz) butter
1 onion, peeled and sliced
1 clove garlic, peeled and crushed
1 teaspoon chopped fresh thyme
225 g (8 oz) flat mushrooms
salt
freshly ground black pepper
1 tablespoon oil
1 tablespoon brandy
300 ml (½ pint) beef stock
15 g (½ oz) butter
15 g (½ oz) plain flour
50 ml (2 fl oz) double or whipping cream
2 teaspoons green peppercorns
sprigs of fresh thyme, to garnish

PREPARATION TIME: 15 minutes, plus
cooling
COOKING TIME: 1¾ hours
OVEN: 160°C, 325°F, Gas Mark 3

1 Cut a pocket in the steak three-quarters of the way through.

2 Melt the butter in a pan, add the onion, garlic and thyme and cook until soft. Add the mushrooms to the pan and cook for 2–3 minutes. Remove the onion, garlic, thyme and mushrooms from the pan and cool.

3 Open up the steak, season both sides with salt and pepper, then stuff it with the onion, garlic and mushrooms. Sew up the steak with fine string. [A]

4 Heat the oil in a frying pan, put in the steak and cook each side for 2–3 minutes until brown. Warm the brandy gently, add to the pan and ignite.

5 When the flames have subsided, add the stock to the pan, bring to the boil then transfer the steak and stock to a shallow casserole. Cover, put into a preheated oven and cook for 1½ hours.

6 Remove the steak from the casserole, remove the string and keep the steak warm.

7 Strain the stock into a saucepan. Mix the butter and flour together and whisk into the stock, off the heat. Bring the stock back to the boil, then stir in the cream and peppercorns. Taste and adjust the seasoning, if necessary, pour the sauce over the steak and garnish with fresh thyme.

[A] The steak can be stuffed up to 1 day in advance. Keep covered and chilled.

CHILLI CON CARNE

175 g (6 oz) pinto beans, soaked overnight
2 tablespoons oil
500 g (1¼ lb) chuck steak, finely diced
1 onion, peeled and chopped
1 small green chilli, seeded and chopped
1 teaspoon dried oregano
1 tablespoon ground cumin
½ teaspoon dried red pepper flakes
1 × 400 g (14 oz) can chopped tomatoes
300 ml (½ pint) beef stock
salt
freshly ground pepper

PREPARATION TIME: 15 minutes, plus
soaking
COOKING TIME: 1¾ hours
OVEN: 160°C, 325°F, Gas Mark 3

1 Put the beans into a pan of cold water, bring to the boil, boil rapidly for 10 minutes, then drain.

2 Heat the oil in a flameproof casserole, add the beef and cook, turning frequently, until browned. Add the onion and green chilli and cook for 2–3 minutes.

3 Add the oregano, cumin, pepper flakes, tomatoes and juice, stock and beans to the casserole, bring to the boil, cover and put into a preheated oven. Cook for 1½ hours, until the beef and beans are tender. Taste and adjust seasoning, if necessary, before serving. [F]

[F] Freeze for up to 3 months. Defrost overnight in the refrigerator or for 4–6 hours at room temperature. Reheat in a saucepan until boiling.

SMOKED FISH CURRY

750 g (1½ lb) smoked haddock, skinned and cut into chunks
2 tablespoons oil
1 onion, peeled and finely chopped
1 clove garlic, peeled and crushed
1 teaspoon turmeric
1 tablespoon mild curry powder
25 g (1 oz) creamed coconut
150 ml (¼ pint) boiling water
1 tablespoon mango chutney
salt
freshly ground black pepper
25 g (1 oz) toasted desiccated coconut

PREPARATION TIME: 10 minutes
COOKING TIME: 30 minutes
OVEN: 180°C, 350°F, Gas Mark 4

Smoked Fish Curry

1 Put the fish into a casserole.

2 Heat the oil in a pan, add the onion and garlic and cook until soft. Add the turmeric and curry powder to the pan and cook for 1 minute.

3 Dissolve the creamed coconut in the water. Add the coconut water and mango chutney to the pan, bring to the boil, add salt and pepper to taste, then pour over the fish. Mix well.

4 Cover the casserole and cook for 25 minutes. Serve sprinkled with the toasted coconut. Plain boiled rice with pistaccio nuts would make a good accompanying dish.

MACKEREL WITH SESAME AND ORANGE

Grated rind and juice of 1 orange
150 ml (¼ pint) water
1 tablespoon soy sauce
15 g (½ oz) butter
1 tablespoon sesame oil
4 large mackerel fillets, approx 175 g (6 oz) each
2 teaspoons cornflour
½ teaspoon ground ginger
salt
freshly ground black pepper
1 tablespoon sesame seeds, to garnish

PREPARATION TIME: 10 minutes
COOKING TIME: 30 minutes
OVEN: 190°C, 375°F, Gas Mark 5

1 Put the orange rind, juice, water and soy sauce into a pan, bring to the boil and simmer for 3 minutes.

2 Heat the butter and sesame oil in a large frying pan and lightly fry the mackerel for 1 minute on each side. Transfer the fish to a shallow casserole, skin side down.

3 Strain the orange juice mixture into the frying pan and reserve the rind.

4 Mix the cornflour with a little water, then add it to the pan with the ginger, salt and pepper. Bring to the boil, then pour over the fish.

5 Cover the casserole, put into a preheated oven and cook for 20 minutes.

6 Serve sprinkled with the reserved orange rind and sesame seeds.

Mackerel with Sesame and Orange

121

ARGENTINE BEEF WITH PEACHES

2 tablespoons oil
450 g (1 lb) chuck steak, diced
1 large onion, peeled and chopped
1 clove garlic, peeled and crushed
1 tablespoon plain flour
300 ml (½ pint) beef stock
150 ml (¼ pint) red wine
1 tablespoon tomato purée
1 teaspoon dried oregano
450 g (1 lb) sweet potatoes, peeled and diced
salt
freshly ground black pepper
3 ripe peaches, skinned and sliced
225 g (8 oz) whole baby sweetcorn or 1 × 450 g
(1 lb) can, drained

PREPARATION TIME: 20 minutes
COOKING TIME: 1 hour 20 minutes
OVEN: 180°C, 350°F, Gas Mark 4

When fresh peaches are not available a 450 g (1 lb) can of peaches in natural juice can be used.

1 Heat the oil in a flameproof casserole. Fry the beef until browned, then add the onion and garlic and cook for 2–3 minutes. Add the flour to the pan and cook for a further minute.

2 Pour in the stock and red wine, then add the tomato purée, oregano, sweet potatoes, salt and pepper and bring to the boil. Cover the casserole, put into a preheated oven and cook for 1 hour.

3 Add the peaches and sweetcorn to the casserole then cook for a further 15 minutes.

From the top: Argentine Beef with Peaches; Sauerbraten; Montego Pepperpot

SAUERBRATEN

SERVES 4–6
85 ml (3 fl oz) red wine
85 ml (3 fl oz) red wine vinegar
1 bay leaf
1 teaspoon dried marjoram
1 teaspoon dried rosemary
1 teaspoon dried thyme
1 teaspoon dried basil
½ teaspoon ground ginger
1 teaspoon juniper berries, crushed
6 black peppercorns
300 ml (½ pint) water
1½ kg (3 lb) lean beef, rolled and tied
25 g (1 oz) butter
1 onion, peeled and chopped
1 carrot, peeled and chopped
1 celery stick
50 g (2 oz) mixed dried fruit
4 ginger snap biscuits
150 ml (5 fl oz) soured cream
salt

PREPARATION TIME: 20 minutes, plus
marinating
COOKING TIME: 3¼–4¼ hours
OVEN: 150°C, 300°F, Gas Mark 2

1 Put the wine, wine vinegar, herbs, spices and water into a pan, bring to the boil then cool.

2 Put the beef into a china or glass bowl, pour over the marinade, cover and marinate for 3–5 days, turning the meat at least once a day.

3 Remove the meat from the marinade and dry it with paper towels. Melt the butter in a flameproof casserole, add the meat and brown it on all sides. Add the onion, carrot, celery and mixed fruit. Strain in the marinade.

4 Bring the liquid to the boil and cover the casserole with foil and a lid. Put into a preheated oven and cook for 3–4 hours, until the beef is tender, turning the meat from time to time.

5 When the meat is cooked, take it out of the casserole, cut it into slices and arrange it on a serving dish. Keep the meat warm.

6 Skim any fat from the top of the liquid in the casserole, then pour the liquid, vegetables and dried fruit into a blender or food processor, add the ginger snaps and blend until smooth. Pour back into the casserole, add the soured cream, and reheat gently without boiling. Taste and adjust the seasoning, if necessary, and pour over the beef.

MONTEGO PEPPERPOT

2 tablespoons oil
450 g (1 lb) shin of beef, diced
1 large onion, peeled and chopped
1 small green chilli, seeds removed and chopped
2 tomatoes, peeled, seeded and diced
1 teaspoon dried thyme
300 ml (½ pint) beef stock
salt
freshly ground black pepper
2 teaspoons Tabasco sauce
450 g (1 lb) yams, peeled and diced
1 × 450 g (1 lb) can red kidney beans, drained

PREPARATION TIME: 15 minutes
COOKING TIME: 2 hours 10 minutes
OVEN: 160°C, 325°F, Gas Mark 3

1 Heat the oil in a pan, add the beef and brown it on all sides. Transfer the beef to a casserole with a slotted spoon. Add the onion and green chilli to the pan and cook until soft.

2 Add the tomatoes, thyme, stock, salt, pepper and Tabasco sauce to the pan and bring to the boil. Add the yams to the casserole, pour the stock over and mix well.

3 Cover the casserole, put into a preheated oven and cook for 1½ hours.

4 Add the kidney beans to the casserole and cook for a further 30 minutes. [F]

[F] Freeze for up to 3 months. Defrost overnight in the refrigerator or for 4–6 hours at room temperature. Reheat at 180°C, 350°F, Gas Mark 4 for 45 minutes.

TURKEY MOLE

15 g (1 oz) lard
750 g (1½ lb) boneless turkey breast, diced
1 onion, peeled and chopped
1 garlic clove, peeled and crushed
300 ml (½ pint) chicken stock
1 small green chilli, seeded and chopped
1 green pepper, cored, seeded and chopped
2 tomatoes, skinned, seeded and chopped
50 g (2 oz) blanched almonds
50 g (2 oz) raisins
1 teaspoon ground coriander
½ teaspoon ground anise or aniseeds
pinch ground cloves
½ teaspoon ground cinnamon
¼ teaspoon dried red pepper flakes
15 g (1 oz) plain chocolate
salt
freshly ground black pepper

PREPARATION TIME: 25 minutes
COOKING TIME: 1¼ hours
OVEN: 180°C, 350°F, Gas Mark 4

1 Melt the lard in a frying pan, fry the turkey, a little at a time, until brown, then transfer it with a slotted spoon to a casserole. Add the onion and garlic to the pan and cook until soft.

2 In a blender or food processor, put the chicken stock, chilli, green pepper, tomatoes, almonds, raisins, spices and red pepper flakes and blend until smooth.

3 Pour into the frying pan, add the chocolate and salt and pepper, and stir until the chocolate has melted. Bring to the boil and cook for 5 minutes. Pour over the turkey and mix well. Cover the casserole, put into a preheated oven, and cook for 1 hour. [F]

[F] Freeze for up to 3 months. Defrost overnight in the refrigerator or for 4–6 hours at room temperature. Reheat at 180°C, 350°F, Gas Mark 4 for 30 minutes.

DUCK FESANJAN

3 pomegranates
chicken stock
1 tablespoon oil
4 boneless duck breasts, about 175 g (6 oz) each,
skinned
1 small onion, peeled and chopped
2 teaspoons lemon juice
½ teaspoon ground cinnamon
pinch chilli powder
1 tablespoon clear honey
salt
freshly ground black pepper

TO GARNISH:
seeds of 1 pomegranate
25 g (1 oz) chopped walnuts

PREPARATION TIME: 15 minutes
COOKING TIME: 50 minutes–1 hour
OVEN: 180°C, 350°F, Gas Mark 4

1 Cut the pomegranates in half, put the seeds into a sieve and push through to extract the juice. Discard the pips and make the pomegranate juice up to 300 ml (½ pint) with the chicken stock.

2 Heat the oil in a frying pan. Fry the duck breasts for 1 minute on each side, then transfer them to a shallow casserole.

3 Add the onion to the pan and cook for 1 minute. Add the pomegranate juice, lemon juice, cinnamon, chilli powder, honey, salt and pepper to the pan, bring to the boil and pour over the duck.

4 Cover the casserole and put into a preheated oven. Cook for 40–50 minutes until the duck is tender.

5 Take the duck breasts out of the casserole with a slotted spoon, place on a warmed serving dish and keep warm.

6 Pour the juices from the casserole into a small saucepan and boil until reduced by half. Pour over the duck and sprinkle with the pomegranate seeds and chopped walnuts.

SPICY BRAISED DUCK

1 × 2¼ kg (5 lb) duck, jointed
small piece cinnamon stick
1 star anise
1 teaspoon whole cardamoms
1 tablespoon oil
1 onion, peeled and chopped
2 garlic cloves, crushed
1 tablespoon grated fresh ginger
2 tablespoons soy sauce
1 tablespoon soft brown sugar
300 ml (½ pint) chicken stock
salt
freshly ground black pepper
spring onion fans, to garnish

PREPARATION TIME: 20 minutes
COOKING TIME: 1¾–2¼ hours
OVEN: 160°C, 325°F, Gas Mark 3

1 Remove the skin and any excess fat and bone from the duck joints, and put them into a casserole with the cinnamon, star anise and cardamoms.

2 Heat the oil in a saucepan, add the onion, garlic and ginger and cook for 2–3 minutes. Add the soy sauce, brown sugar, chicken stock, salt and pepper to the pan, bring to the boil, pour over the duck and cover the casserole. Put into a preheated oven and cook for 1½–2 hours, turning the duck from time to time, until the duck is quite tender.

3 When the duck is cooked, take it out of the casserole with a slotted spoon, put on a serving dish and keep warm.

4 Pour the liquid through a sieve into a saucepan, discarding the cinnamon, star anise, and cardamoms. Push the onion, garlic and ginger through the sieve, reheat the sauce, reducing it a little, if necessary, to achieve a coating consistency. Pour over the duck.

5 Garnish the duck with the spring onion fans.

Clockwise from top: Turkey Mole; Duck Fesanjan; Spicy Braised Duck

PRAWNS AND OKRA IN COCONUT SAUCE

2 tablespoons oil
1 small onion, finely chopped
1 small green pepper, wiped clean and finely chopped
450 g (1 lb) small, even-sized okra, stalk end removed
50 g (2 oz) creamed coconut
300 ml (½ pint) boiling water
1 tablespoon chilli sauce
1 tablespoon tomato purée
salt
freshly ground black pepper
225 g (8 oz) peeled prawns

PREPARATION TIME: 15 minutes
COOKING TIME: 45 minutes
OVEN: 180°C, 350°F, Gas Mark 4

Clockwise from top: Prawns and Okra in Coconut Sauce; Chinese Crab and Rice Casserole; Baccala

1 Heat the oil in a flameproof casserole, add the onion and green pepper and cook until soft. Add the okra to the casserole and cook for a further minute.

2 Dissolve the creamed coconut in the boiling water, then add the chilli sauce, tomato purée, salt and pepper.

3 Pour the coconut mixture into the casserole, bring to the boil, cover and put into a preheated oven. Cook for 30 minutes.

4 Add the prawns to the casserole, mixing them well in. Cook the casserole, covered, for a further 10 minutes.

CHINESE CRAB AND RICE CASSEROLE

1 tablespoon oil
1 onion, peeled and chopped
2 celery sticks, sliced
350 g (12 oz) cooked long-grain rice
50 g (2 oz) frozen peas
1 × 225 g (8 oz) can water chestnuts, drained
225 g (8 oz) crabmeat
25 g (1 oz) butter
50 g (2 oz) blanched almonds
150 ml (1/4 pint) tomato juice
1 tablespoon light soy sauce
salt
freshly ground black pepper

PREPARATION TIME: 15 minutes
COOKING TIME: 35 minutes
OVEN: 180°C, 350°F, Gas Mark 4

1 Heat the oil in a pan, add the onion and celery and cook until soft, then add to the rice in a mixing bowl with the peas, water chestnuts and crabmeat.

2 Melt the butter in a pan, fry the almonds until lightly browned, then add the almonds, butter, tomato juice, soy sauce, salt and pepper to the rice mixture and mix well.

3 Put the mixture into a casserole. Cover, put into a preheated oven and cook for 25 minutes.

BACCALA

450 g (1 lb) salt cod
2 tablespoons olive oil
1 onion, peeled and chopped
1 green pepper, cored, seeded and chopped
1 garlic clove, peeled and crushed
1 × 400 g (14 oz) can chopped tomatoes, juice reserved
2 tablespoons chopped fresh parsley
salt
freshly ground black pepper
450 g (1 lb) cooked potatoes, sliced
2 hard-boiled eggs, shelled and cut into wedges, to garnish

PREPARATION TIME: 15 minutes, plus soaking
COOKING TIME: 1½ hours
OVEN: 180°C, 350°F, Gas Mark 4

If salt cod is unavailable, use 450 g (1 lb) fresh cod. Omit the initial soaking, then proceed with the recipe.

1 Soak the cod in cold water for 24 hours, changing the water 3 or 4 times.

2 Drain the fish and put into fresh cold water, bring to the boil then simmer for 15–20 minutes, until the fish flakes easily. Drain, then leave until cool enough to handle. Skin, bone and flake the fish. [A]

3 Heat the oil in a pan, add the onion, pepper and garlic and cook for 2 minutes. Add the tomatoes and their juice, parsley, a little salt and the pepper, bring to the boil, then add the fish.

4 Layer the potatoes and fish mixture in a casserole, starting with potatoes and ending with fish. Cover the casserole, put into a preheated oven and cook for 1 hour.

5 Serve garnished with the wedges of hard-boiled egg.

[A] The fish can be cooked up to 1 day in advance. Keep covered and chilled.

GOAN PORK

120 ml (4 fl oz) white wine vinegar
1 teaspoon ground cumin
1 teaspoon ground chilli
1 teaspoon cardamom seeds
1 teaspoon ground cinnamon
1 teaspoon ground coriander
½ teaspoon ground turmeric
750 g (1½ lb) lean pork, diced
3-4 tablespoons mustard oil
1 large onion, peeled and sliced
1 teaspoon grated fresh ginger
3 cloves garlic, peeled and crushed
1 small green chilli, seeded and chopped
300 ml (½ pint) water
salt
freshly ground black pepper

PREPARATION TIME: 15 minutes, plus
marinating time
COOKING TIME: 1 hour 10 minutes–1 hour
20 minutes
OVEN: 180°C, 350°F, Gas Mark 4

Mustard oil is available in health food shops.

1 Mix the vinegar and spices together in a glass or ceramic bowl, add the pork, mix well, cover and leave in a cool place or refrigerator for 24 hours.

2 Heat the oil in a pan, add the onion, ginger, garlic and green chilli and cook until softened. Transfer to a casserole with a slotted spoon.

3 Drain the meat, reserving the marinade. Dry the meat on paper towels and fry it, a little at a time, in the pan, until brown, then add to the casserole.

4 Put the marinade into the pan with the water, bring to the boil, add the salt and pepper and pour over the meat. Cover the casserole, put into a preheated oven and cook for 1–1¼ hours until the meat is tender, stirring from time to time. [F]

[F] Freeze for up to 3 months, defrost overnight in the refrigerator or for 4–6 hours at room temperature. Reheat at 180°C, 350°F, Gas Mark 4 for 40 minutes.

SWEET AND SOUR PORK HONG KONG STYLE

2-3 tablespoons oil
1 large onion, peeled and chopped
1 large green pepper, cored, seeded and chopped
1 garlic clove, peeled and crushed
500 g (1¼ lb) lean pork, diced
3 tablespoons cornflour
1 × 425 g (15 oz) can lychees in syrup
2 tablespoons wine vinegar
1 tablespoon soft brown sugar
1 tablespoon tomato ketchup
2 tablespoons soy sauce
salt
freshly ground black pepper

PREPARATION TIME: 15 minutes
COOKING TIME: 1¼ hours
OVEN: 180°C, 350°F, Gas Mark 4

1 Heat the oil in a frying pan, add the onion, pepper and garlic and cook until soft. Transfer to a casserole with a slotted spoon.

2 Coat the pork in 2 tablespoons of the cornflour and fry in the oil until brown. Add the pork to the casserole.

3 Drain the syrup from the lychees: there should be about 250 ml (8 fl oz). Mix the syrup with the vinegar, brown sugar, tomato ketchup, soy sauce, salt and pepper and the remaining cornflour.

4 Mix well, then pour into the pan, bring to the boil and strain into the casserole.

5 Cover the casserole, put into a preheated oven and cook for 1 hour. [F]

6 Add the lychees to the casserole and cook for a further 10 minutes.

[F] Freeze for up to 3 months, defrost overnight in the refrigerator or for 4–6 hours at room temperature. Reheat at 180°C, 350°F, Gas Mark 4 for 20 minutes, then proceed as above.

CALYPSO PORK

*2 tablespoons oil
1 onion, peeled and sliced
1 clove garlic, peeled and crushed
4 pork chops, approx 225 g (8 oz) each, rind
removed
2 tablespoons rum
1 teaspoon ground ginger
3 tablespoons guava jelly
1 tablespoon cornflour
85 ml (3 fl oz) water
salt
freshly ground black pepper
1 guava, peeled and sliced, to garnish*

PREPARATION TIME: 15 minutes
COOKING TIME: 55 minutes
OVEN: 190°C, 375°F, Gas Mark 5

If guava jelly is not available, any clear yellow fruit jelly would make an acceptable substitute in this recipe.

1 Heat the oil in a frying pan, add the onion and garlic and cook until soft, then transfer to a casserole.

2 Put the pork chops into the frying pan and cook for 2 minutes on each side. Pour the rum into the pan, then ignite. When the flames have subsided, transfer the chops to the casserole.

3 Add the ginger and guava jelly to the pan and stir gently until the jelly has melted.

4 Mix the cornflour with the water, pour into the pan, bring to the boil, season with salt and pepper, then pour over the chops.

5 Cover the casserole and cook for 45 minutes. Serve garnished with the sliced guava.

From the top: Goan Pork; Sweet and Sour Pork Hong Kong Style; Calypso Pork

PORK AVGOLEMONO

2 tablespoons oil
1 large onion, peeled and chopped
500 g (1¼ lb) lean pork, diced
25 g (1 oz) plain flour
150 ml (¼ pint) dry white wine
300 ml (½ pint) light stock
450 g (1 lb) celeriac, peeled and diced
salt
freshly ground black pepper
2 egg yolks
2 tablespoons lemon juice
1 tablespoon chopped fresh parsley

PREPARATION TIME: 20 minutes
COOKING TIME: 1 hour 10 minutes–1 hour 25 minutes
OVEN: 180°C, 350°F, Gas Mark 4

Clockwise from top:
Pork Avgolemono;
Puchero; Jambalaya

1 Heat the oil in a flameproof casserole. Add the onion and pork and fry gently for 2–3 minutes.

2 Stir the flour into the casserole, cook for 1 minute then add the wine, stock, celeriac, salt and pepper. Bring to the boil, cover the casserole, put into a preheated oven and cook for 1–1½ hours until the pork is tender. [F]

3 Remove the casserole from the oven and put back on to the heat. Mix together the egg yolks, lemon juice and parsley. Add 3 tablespoons of stock from the casserole. Pour the sauce back into the casserole, stir well and reheat gently, but do not boil.

[F] Freeze for up to 3 months. Defrost overnight in the refrigerator or for 4–6 hours at room temperature. Reheat at 180°C, 350°F, Gas Mark 4 for 30 minutes, then proceed as in the recipe.

PUCHERO

2 tablespoons oil
1 onion, peeled and chopped
1 clove garlic, peeled and crushed
225 g (8 oz) carrots, peeled and diced
1 × 400 g (14 oz) can tomatoes
1 tablespoon wine vinegar
150 ml (¼ pint) water
1 bay leaf
½ teaspoon crushed dried red chillis
500 g (1¼ lb) piece salt pork, boned, rinded and
soaked overnight
175 g (6 oz) chorizo sausage
1 × 450 g (1 lb) can red kidney beans, drained
sprigs of fresh rosemary, to garnish

PREPARATION TIME: 15 minutes, plus
soaking
COOKING TIME: 2 hours 40 minutes
OVEN: 180°C, 350°F, Gas Mark 4

1 Heat the oil in a pan, add the onion, garlic and carrots and cook for 2–3 minutes.

2 Add the tomatoes and juice to the pan, then add the vinegar, water, bay leaf and crushed chillis. Bring to the boil.

3 Put the salt pork into a casserole. Pour the sauce over, cover, put into a preheated oven and cook for 2 hours.

4 Add the chorizo sausage and beans to the casserole and cook for a further 30 minutes.

5 To serve, remove the pork and sausage from the casserole, slice them and put them on to a warmed serving dish. Remove the bay leaf and pour the sauce over the meats, garnishing the dish with fresh rosemary.

JAMBALAYA

3 tablespoons oil
1 large onion, peeled and sliced
1 large green pepper, seeded, cored and sliced
1 large red pepper, seeded, cored and sliced
1 clove garlic, peeled and crushed
225 g (8 oz) long-grain rice
600 ml (1 pint) hot chicken stock
225 g (8 oz) piece cooked ham, diced
salt
freshly ground black pepper
4 tomatoes, skinned, seeded and cut into strips
225 g (8 oz) peeled prawns

TO GARNISH:
8 whole prawns
sprigs of fresh parsley

PREPARATION TIME: 15 minutes
COOKING TIME: 1 hour
OVEN: 190°C, 375°F, Gas Mark 5

1 Heat the oil in a flameproof casserole, add the onion, peppers and garlic and cook for 2–3 minutes.

2 Add the rice to the pan, and stir around until all the grains are coated with the oil. Pour in the stock, add the ham and salt and pepper, bring to the boil then cover the casserole with foil and a lid. Put into a preheated oven and cook for 45 minutes.

3 Remove the casserole from the oven. There should be just a little liquid left; if not, add 2 or 3 tablespoons stock, then add the tomatoes and prawns. Recover the casserole, put back into the oven and cook for a further 10–15 minutes, until the prawns and tomatoes are heated through and all the liquid has been absorbed.

4 Serve garnished with the whole prawns and fresh parsley.

VEAL STIFADO

2 tablespoons olive oil
500 g (1¼ lb) pie veal, diced
1 clove garlic, peeled and crushed
450 g (1 lb) button onions, peeled and blanched
1 tablespoon plain flour
1 teaspoon ground cinnamon
1 tablespoon red wine vinegar
150 ml (¼ pint) red wine
3 tablespoons tomato purée
150 ml (¼ pint) water
½ teaspoon dried oregano
salt
freshly ground black pepper

PREPARATION TIME: 15 minutes
COOKING TIME: 1 hour 35 minutes
OVEN: 180°C, 350°F, Gas Mark 4

Veal Stifado

1 Heat the oil in a flameproof casserole, add the veal, garlic and onions and cook for 2–3 minutes.

2 Stir in the flour and cook for a further minute, then add the cinnamon, red wine vinegar, red wine, tomato purée, water, oregano, salt and pepper. Bring to the boil, stirring well.

3 Cover the casserole, put into a preheated oven and cook for about 1½ hours, until the veal and onions are tender. [F]

[F] Freeze for up to 3 months. Defrost overnight in the refrigerator or for 4–6 hours at room temperature. Reheat at 180°C, 350°F, Gas Mark 4 for 35–40 minutes.

ELIZABETHAN RABBIT

1 rabbit, approx 1¼ kg (2½ lb), jointed
1 tablespoon seasoned flour
2-3 tablespoons oil
1 dessert apple, peeled, cored and sliced
100 g (4 oz) seedless green grapes
50 g (2¼ oz) raisins
1 orange, segmented
grated rind and juice of 1 orange
1 bouquet garni
1 onion, peeled and chopped
2 sticks celery, sliced
150 ml (¼ pint) red wine
85 ml (3 fl oz) chicken stock
salt
freshly ground black pepper
fine strips of orange rind, to garnish

PREPARATION TIME: 20 minutes
COOKING TIME: 2 hours 10 minutes
OVEN: 160°C, 325°F, Gas Mark 3

1 Coat the rabbit with the seasoned flour.

2 Heat the oil in a frying pan and fry the rabbit joints until lightly browned. Transfer to a casserole, then put the apple, grapes, raisins, orange segments, orange rind and juice and bouquet garni into the casserole.

3 Add the onion and celery to the frying pan with a little extra oil, if necessary, and cook for 2–3 minutes. Add the wine and stock to the pan, bring to the boil and pour over the rabbit. Cover the casserole, put into a preheated oven and cook for 2 hours until the rabbit is very tender.

4 Taste and adjust the seasoning, if necessary, and remove the bouquet garni before serving garnished with strips of orange rind.

Elizabethan Rabbit

PARTY
PIECES

Here is where to find those special celebration-time recipes: casseroles to make an impression or to get a party going, casseroles to feed a crowd and casseroles to make the memorable centrepiece of an elegant dinner party. Some of the recipes, such as the Seafood and Wild Rice Casserole or the Vegetable-Braised Veal Roast, are undeniably expensive, but they are intended for very special, once-in-a-lifetime occasions; others, like the Pork Ribs Casserole with Chilli Biscuits and the Tex-Mex Chilli are guaranteed to add spice to any gathering. While some of the casseroles are quite complicated to prepare, others are deceptively simple, while many can be made the day before, to be reheated easily and served without fuss at the party.

BRAISED STUFFED SHOULDER OF LAMB

SERVES 6

FOR THE STUFFING:
50 g (2 oz) butter
75 g (3 oz) mushrooms, cleaned and sliced
1 small onion, peeled and finely chopped
100 g (4 oz) crustless day-old white bread, diced
75 g (3 oz) pine nuts
25 g (1 oz) chopped fresh parsley
2 sticks celery, finely chopped
2 eggs, beaten
1 tablespoon chopped fresh tarragon or 1 teaspoon dried tarragon
1 tablespoon chopped fresh mint or 1 teaspoon dried mint
½ teaspoon paprika
salt
freshly ground black pepper

FOR THE LAMB:
2 garlic cloves, peeled and cut into slivers
1 × 1½ kg (3¼ lb) shoulder of lamb, boned, pocket cut and the bones reserved
1 tablespoon rosemary leaves or ½ teaspoon dried rosemary
salt
freshly ground black pepper
3 tablespoons vegetable oil
475 ml (16 fl oz) lamb or beef stock
50 g (2 oz) onion, peeled and diced
50 g (2 oz) carrots, peeled and diced
25 g (1 oz) celery, diced
150 g (5 oz) potatoes, peeled and diced
2 tablespoons cornflour
50 ml (2 fl oz) port
50 ml (2 fl oz) lamb or beef stock
4 sprigs fresh mint, to garnish

PREPARATION TIME: 45 minutes
COOKING TIME: 2½ hours
OVEN: 160°C, 325°F, Gas Mark 3

The amount of bread needed for this stuffing may have to be altered, depending on the bread you use. The 100 g (4 oz) of crustless diced bread used in this recipe was, in fact, 12 slices of white bread. A simple way of determining if you have the correct amount of diced bread is to put it into a pint measuring jug: if you have just over a pint, you will have enough to make the required amount of stuffing.

The lamb shoulder must be boned. When it is boned, you will find that there is a 'pocket' in the centre of the shoulder. Cut the pocket to extend it almost, but not through, the shoulder. One end of the shoulder should still be intact. The stuffing will then be placed in the pocket.

1 For the stuffing, melt the butter in a large frying pan over a medium heat. Add the onion and mushrooms then cook for 10 minutes, stirring frequently. Remove the mixture from the heat and tip into a large glass or ceramic bowl.

2 Add the remaining ingredients for the stuffing, then stir gently until well combined. Set aside. [A]

3 Insert the slivers of garlic under the skin of the lamb. Lay the lamb out flat, skin side down, on a working surface. Place the stuffing evenly in the pocket of the shoulder. Close the open end of the shoulder with 4 metal skewers. Roll the meat to tuck the long ends of the roast underneath, then tie firmly with string. Sprinkle the roast with the rosemary, salt and pepper.

4 Heat the oil in a large frying pan over a medium heat. Place the roast in the frying pan. Brown on all sides, using 2 large spoons to turn the roast. Remove the roast from the pan and set aside.

5 Pour 250 ml (8 fl oz) of the stock into a large casserole. Add the roast and the reserved bones. Cover and place in a preheated oven. Cook for 45 minutes.

6 Remove the casserole from the oven, then add the remaining stock, onions, carrots, celery and potatoes. Cover and return to the oven. Cook for 1 hour.

7 Remove the casserole from the oven. Transfer the roast to a heated platter and keep warm. Discard the bones from the sauce, then skim off the fat.

8 Bring the sauce to the boil in a large saucepan over a high heat. Thoroughly combine the cornflour, port and stock in a large cup. Whisk into the sauce then cook for 4–5 minutes, stirring constantly, until thick and smooth. Strain the sauce into a heated sauceboat.

9 To serve, place the roast on a heated serving platter and garnish with the mint. Serve the sauce separately. Serve with boiled new potatoes and a coloured vegetable, such as mangetout or baby sweetcorn.

LAMB SHREWSBURY

SERVES 6
50 g (2 oz) plain flour
1 tablespoon finely chopped fresh rosemary or
½ teaspoon dried rosemary
salt
freshly ground black pepper
6 × 175 g (6 oz) loin lamb chops
50 g (2 oz) butter
1 onion, peeled and finely chopped
1 carrot, peeled and sliced
1 large tomato, peeled, seeded and diced
1 garlic clove, peeled and finely chopped
2 tablespoons tomato purée
120 ml (4 fl oz) port wine
900 ml (1½ pints) beef stock
4 tablespoons redcurrant jelly
1 bunch watercress, to garnish

PREPARATION TIME: 15 minutes
COOKING TIME: 1½ hours
OVEN: 180°C, 350°F, Gas Mark 4

1 Combine the flour, rosemary, salt and pepper and coat the chops in the mixture.

2 Heat the butter in a large flameproof casserole over a moderate heat. Add the chops and brown on one side for 5 minutes. Turn the chops over and continue to brown for 5 minutes.

3 Add the onion, carrot, tomato and garlic to the casserole. Blend in the tomato purée, port, stock and redcurrant jelly. Cover and place in a preheated oven. Cook for 1 hour. [A]

4 Remove the chops from the sauce and place on a heated serving platter. Strain the sauce and return to the cleaned casserole. Simmer for 10 minutes over a moderate heat until thick.

5 To serve, pour the sauce over the chops and garnish with the watercress.

[A] The casserole may be made one day in advance, covered and kept chilled. Simmer for 10–20 minutes, until heated through.

From the left: Braised Stuffed Shoulder of Lamb; Lamb Shrewsbury

TEX-MEX CHILLI WITH THE FIXINGS

SERVES 6

FOR THE CHILLI:
1 kg (2 lb) braising steak, trimmed and cut into
2.5 cm (1 inch cubes)
5 tablespoons vegetable oil
4 tablespoons mild or mild-hot chilli powder
3 medium onions, peeled and finely chopped
4 garlic cloves, peeled and finely chopped
1 tablespoon dried oregano
2 teaspoons ground cumin
salt
freshly ground black pepper
4 × 400 g (14 oz) cans tomatoes, drained and
chopped
750 ml (1¼ pints) lager
175 g (6 oz) tomato purée
2 tablespoons red wine vinegar
2 × 400 g (14 oz) cans kidney beans, drained

SALSA:
3 large tomatoes, peeled, cored, seeded and diced
50 ml (2 fl oz) lemon juice
25 ml (1 fl oz) lime juice
1 small onion, peeled and finely chopped
2 tablespoons finely chopped fresh coriander
1 large garlic clove, peeled and finely chopped
2-4 green chillies, seeded, pith removed and minced
salt
freshly ground black pepper

TO GARNISH:
250 ml (8 fl oz) soured cream
1 large avocado pear, halved, peeled and sliced
lime twists
100 g (4 oz) Cheddar cheese, grated
8 spring onions, finely chopped
16-24 corn tortillas, heated

PREPARATION TIME: 1½ hours, plus
marinating
COOKING TIME: 4 hours
OVEN: 180°C, 350°F, Gas Mark 4

1 For the chilli, coat the meat well in 3 tablespoons of the oil and 3 tablespoons of the chilli powder. Cover and chill overnight.

2 Heat the remaining oil in a large frying pan over a medium heat. Add the beef and brown on all sides for 5 minutes. Transfer the meat to a large flameproof casserole.

3 Add the onions to the frying pan. Cook over a medium heat for 10 minutes until soft and golden. Stir in the garlic, remaining chilli powder, oregano, cumin, salt and pepper.

Cook for 5 minutes, stirring frequently. Remove from the heat and blend the onion mixture into the meat.

4 Stir the tomatoes, lager, tomato purée and vinegar into the meat mixture. Place the casserole over a medium-high heat and bring to the boil. Cover and transfer to a preheated oven. Cook for 3 hours, stirring occasionally.

5 Stir the beans into the chilli. Continue cooking, uncovered, for 30 minutes. [A]

6 Now make the salsa. Blend together the tomatoes, lemon and lime juice, onion, coriander, garlic, chillies, salt and pepper in a bowl. Transfer to a serving dish and set aside. [A]

7 Now skim the fat from the casserole. Simmer over a low heat until heated through. Taste and correct the seasoning, if necessary.

8 Garnish each serving with soured cream, slices of avocado and lime twist. Serve with the salsa, cheese, spring onions and tortillas.

[A] The chilli can be made a day in advance, covered and kept chilled. Simmer for 10–20 minutes before bringing to the boil. The salsa can be made several hours in advance.

VENISON STEAKS BRAISED IN RED WINE

SERVES 6

FOR THE MARINADE:
475 ml (16 fl oz) red wine
120 ml (4 fl oz) red wine vinegar
100 g (4 oz) leeks, white part only, sliced
100 g (4 oz) onions, peeled and diced
75 g (3 oz) carrots, peeled and diced
2 garlic cloves, peeled and crushed
1 bay leaf
1 tablespoon fresh thyme or
½ teaspoon dried thyme
1 tablespoon finely chopped fresh tarragon
salt
freshly ground black pepper
6 × 175 g (6 oz) venison steaks, trimmed of all fat

TO COOK THE VENISON:
75 g (3 oz) butter
75 g (3 oz) plain flour
900 ml (1½ pints) strong beef stock
1 tablespoon vegetable oil
2 tablespoons redcurrant jelly
120 ml (4 fl oz) double or whipping cream
1 bunch watercress, to garnish

PREPARATION TIME: 45 minutes, plus
cooling and marinating
COOKING TIME: 1¾ hours
OVEN: 180°C, 350°F, Gas Mark 4

1 Combine all the ingredients for the marinade, except the venison steaks, in a large saucepan. Bring to the boil over a high heat. Boil for 2 minutes, then remove from the heat. Let cool for 15 minutes.

2 Place the venison steaks in a single layer in a large, shallow casserole. Pour the warm marinade over the steaks, then cover. Marinate for at least 4 hours, preferably overnight, turning the meat frequently.

3 Remove the steaks from the marinade, cover and set aside. Melt 50 g (2 oz) of the butter in a large saucepan over a moderate heat. Blend in the flour and, stirring constantly, cook for 2–3 minutes. Using a whisk, gradually stir in the unstrained marinade and stock. Bring to the boil. Reduce the heat and simmer gently for 30 minutes. Strain the sauce through a fine sieve, pressing hard on the vegetables. Set aside.

4 Heat the remaining butter and oil in a large flameproof casserole over a medium heat. Sprinkle the steaks with salt and pepper. Place the steaks in the casserole and brown on one side for 4–5 minutes. Turn the steaks over and brown on the other side for 3–4 minutes.

Remove the steaks from the casserole with a slotted spoon or tongs. Drain the fat from the casserole and discard. Return the steaks to the casserole and add the sauce. [A] Cover and place in a preheated oven. Cook for 30 minutes.

5 Remove the casserole from the oven. Transfer the steaks to a heated platter and keep warm. Place the casserole on a high heat and bring to the boil, stirring occasionally. Boil for 5 minutes. Strain the sauce through a fine sieve and return to a clean saucepan. Add the redcurrant jelly, cream, salt and pepper to taste, then return to the boil. Remove from the heat.

6 To serve, spoon a tablespoon of the sauce over each steak. Garnish with the watercress. Transfer the remaining sauce to a sauceboat and serve. Sautéed potato balls and a carrot purée would be good side dishes.

[A] The casserole may be made several hours in advance, covered and kept chilled. Bring the casserole to a simmer before proceeding with the recipe.

From the left: Tex-Mex Chilli with the Fixings; Venison Steaks Braised in Red Wine

PORK RIBS CASSEROLE WITH CHILLI BISCUITS

SERVES 6
1½ kg (3 lb) lean pork spareribs

FOR THE SAUCE:
3 tablespoons vegetable oil
1 large onion, peeled and finely chopped
4 garlic cloves, peeled and finely chopped
2 × 400 g (14 oz) cans tomatoes
475 ml (16 fl oz) beef stock
85 ml (3 fl oz) cider vinegar
50 g (2 oz) demerara sugar
3 tablespoons Worcestershire sauce
2 tablespoons Dijon mustard
2 tablespoons lemon juice
1 teaspoon chopped fresh parsley
½ teaspoon paprika
½ teaspoon ground turmeric
¼ teaspoon cayenne pepper
salt
freshly ground black pepper

FOR THE CHILLI BISCUITS:
15 g (½ oz) butter
1 medium onion, peeled and finely chopped
1 garlic clove, peeled and finely chopped
350 g (12 oz) plain flour
1 tablespoon baking powder
2 teaspoons mild chilli powder
salt
50 g (2 oz) freshly grated Parmesan cheese
2 tablespoons finely chopped fresh coriander
50 g (2 oz) well-chilled lard, cubed
175 ml (6 fl oz) milk

PREPARATION TIME: 30 minutes
COOKING TIME: 2½ hours
OVEN: 190°C, 375°F, Gas Mark 5;
then: 230°C, 450°F, Gas Mark 8

1 Arrange the ribs in a single layer in a large, shallow roasting pan. Grill under a preheated grill, turning frequently, until brown.

2 For the sauce, heat the oil in a large flameproof casserole over a medium heat. Add the onion and garlic, then cook for 10 minutes. Blend in the remaining ingredients for the sauce. Add the ribs. Cover the casserole and cook in a preheated oven for 1¾ hours until the ribs are tender. [A] [F]

3 For the biscuits, melt the butter in a medium frying pan over a moderate heat. Add the onion and garlic, then cook for 10 minutes, stirring frequently. Allow the mixture to cool for 10 minutes.

4 Sift the flour, baking powder, chilli powder and salt into a large bowl. Stir in the cheese and coriander. Cut in the lard until the mixture resembles coarse crumbs. Blend in the onion mixture. Make a well in the centre of the flour mixture, pour in the milk and mix with a fork just until the dough comes together. Turn the dough out on to a lightly floured surface and knead 5 times. Roll the dough out to a 1 cm (½ inch) thickness. Using a 7.5 cm (3 inch) floured cutter, cut out 6–8 biscuits and place on a baking sheet.

5 When the ribs have cooked for 1¾ hours, take off the cover. Increase the oven heat to 230°C, 450°F, Gas Mark 8. Put the biscuits in the oven. Bake for 12–15 minutes, until the biscuits are puffed and lightly browned.

6 Arrange the biscuits around the ribs.

[A] Can be prepared 2 days in advance, covered and chilled. Bring the ribs to a simmer for 10 minutes before proceeding with the recipe.

[F] Can be prepared 1 month in advance. Allow the ribs to cool down before freezing. Bring the ribs to a simmer for 10 minutes before continuing with the recipe.

PORK MEDLEY

SERVES 6

FOR THE PORK:
12 pork medallions, about 2.5 cm (1 inch) thick
300 ml (½ pint) dry cider
4 tablespoons plain flour
salt
freshly ground black pepper
2 tablespoons vegetable oil
225 g (8 oz) button mushrooms, cleaned and halved
1 large onion, peeled and chopped
1 green pepper, cored, seeded and chopped
2 tomatoes, cored and quartered
1 garlic clove, peeled and finely chopped

FOR THE SAUCE:
40 g (1½ oz) butter
3 tablespoons plain flour
250 ml (8 fl oz) beef stock
1 tablespoon fresh thyme or 1 teaspoon dried thyme
120 ml (4 fl oz) double cream
4 sprigs parsley

PREPARATION TIME: 30 minutes, plus marinating
COOKING TIME: 1¼ hours
OVEN: 180°C, 350°F, Gas Mark 4

1 Place the medallions and cider in a large, shallow dish. Cover and chill overnight.

2 Remove the medallions from the cider with a slotted spoon and pat dry. Reserve the cider. Combine 2 tablespoons of the flour, salt and pepper, on a large plate. Toss the medallions in the flour mixture, coating well. Set aside.

3 Heat the oil in a large frying pan over a high heat. When the pan is hot, but not smoking, add the medallions. Cook for 2–3 minutes, shaking the pan frequently to prevent sticking, until the medallions are browned. Turn the meat over and continue cooking for another 2–3 minutes. Remove the meat from the pan and place in a large flameproof casserole. Surround the medallions with the mushrooms, onion, green pepper, tomatoes and garlic.

4 For the sauce, melt the butter in the frying pan over a moderate heat. Blend in the flour and cook for 2–3 minutes, stirring frequently. Using a whisk, gradually add the stock. Bring the mixture to a simmer, stirring continuously. Cook for 2–3 minutes until the sauce is thick and smooth. Blend in the reserved cider and thyme. Pour the sauce over the medallions, then cover. [A] Cook in a preheated oven for 45 minutes until the pork is tender.

5 Transfer the medallions to a heated serving platter. Remove the vegetables with a slotted spoon and arrange around the medallions.

6 Heat the sauce in the casserole over a high heat. Stir in the cream, then taste and correct the seasoning, if necessary. Pour the sauce over the medallions and garnish with the parsley sprigs. Serve immediately.

[A] The casserole can be made earlier in the day, covered and chilled. Simmer for 10 minutes before proceeding with the recipe.

From the left: Pork Ribs Casserole with Chilli Biscuits; Pork Medley

VEGETABLE-BRAISED VEAL ROAST

SERVES 8
65 g (3 oz) butter
1 × 2¼ kg (5 lb) loin of veal, trimmed of fat, boned, tenderloin and kidneys replaced evenly inside the loin, rolled and tied
3 carrots, peeled and cut into julienne strips
3 leeks, white part only, cut into julienne strips
1 large tomato, peeled, seeded and diced
1 large garlic clove, peeled and finely chopped
salt
freshly ground white pepper
½ tablespoon fresh thyme leaves or ½ teaspoon dried thyme
475 ml (16 fl oz) veal or chicken stock
250 ml (8 fl oz) dry white wine
1½ tablespoons cornflour
50 ml (2 fl oz) dry sherry
4 sprigs watercress, to garnish

PREPARATION TIME: 35–45 minutes
COOKING TIME: 2¾ hours
OVEN: 180°C, 350°F, Gas Mark 4

Ask the butcher to prepare the veal roast. The loin must be trimmed of most of its fat and boned. (Ask for the bones – they make a good stock.) The tenderloin and kidneys are then placed inside the loin where the bones used to be. Finally, the roast is rolled and tied with string.

1 Melt 50 g (2 oz) of the butter in a large flameproof casserole over a medium heat. Place the roast in the casserole, then brown on all sides, using 2 large spoons to turn the roast. Remove the roast from the casserole and set aside.

2 Add the carrots and leeks to the casserole. Cook, stirring frequently, for 2 minutes. Lower the heat, then add the tomato, garlic, thyme, salt and pepper. Cook gently for 2 minutes, stirring occasionally. Remove the casserole from the heat and set aside to cool for a few minutes.

3 Cut a piece of greaseproof paper 40 cm × 40 cm (16 inches × 16 inches). Lay the paper on a working surface, then coat with the remaining butter. Spread half of the vegetable mixture evenly on the paper. Place the roast in the centre of the vegetables. Coat the roast with the remaining vegetables. Bring up the sides of the paper to enclose the roast, then fold the top securely. Fold the sides securely underneath the roast. Return the wrapped roast to the casserole. [A] Pour the stock and wine over the roast

and place the casserole on the stove. Bring to the boil over a medium heat, then cover. Transfer the casserole to a preheated oven, then cook for 2 hours, until the juices run clear when the roast is pricked with a skewer.

4 Remove the roast from the casserole and place on a heated platter. Place the casserole over a medium heat on the stove. Combine the cornflour and sherry in a cup until smooth. Whisk into the casserole, then bring the sauce to the boil, stirring constantly. Add salt and pepper to taste.

5 Unwrap the roast and cut the strings off. Add the vegetables and juices from the roast to the sauce. Return the sauce to the boil.

6 To serve, slice the roast and place on a heated serving platter. Coat the slices with the sauce, then garnish with the watercress. Serve with creamed potatoes, buttered French green beans and grilled stuffed tomatoes.

STUFFED VEAL ROLLS

FOR THE STUFFING:
40 g (1½ oz) butter
450 g (1 lb) lean minced pork
1 small onion, peeled and finely chopped
1 celery stalk, finely chopped
75 g (3 oz) field mushrooms, cleaned and chopped
1 garlic clove, peeled and finely chopped
2 tablespoons finely chopped fresh parsley
salt
freshly ground black pepper
8 veal escalopes, about 50 g (2 oz) each and 15 cm (6 inches) wide

FOR THE SAUCE:
50 g (2 oz) butter
2 medium onions, peeled and thinly sliced
1 garlic clove, peeled and finely chopped
250 ml (8 fl oz) dry white wine
275 ml (9 fl oz) beef stock
2 teaspoons cornflour
1 tablespoon chopped fresh parsley, to garnish

PREPARATION TIME: 30 minutes
COOKING TIME: 1¾ hours
OVEN: 180°C, 350°F, Gas Mark 4

1 Melt 15 g (½ oz) of the butter in a large frying pan over a moderate heat. Add the pork then, stirring frequently, cook for 10 minutes until browned. Remove the pork to a medium bowl with a slotted spoon and set aside.

2 Melt 25 g (1 oz) of the butter in the frying

pan over a moderate heat. Add the onion, celery, mushrooms and garlic. Cook for 10 minutes, stirring frequently. Remove from the heat. Blend into the cooked pork. Stir in the parsley, salt and pepper, then set aside.

3 Lay the escalopes on a working surface. Place 2 tablespoons of the stuffing on one end of each escalope. Roll up to enclose the stuffing, then tie securely with string. [A]

4 Melt 25 g (1 oz) of the sauce butter in a large flameproof casserole over a medium–high heat. Add the veal rolls and, turning frequently, cook for 5 minutes, until browned on all sides. Remove the casserole from the heat and set aside.

5 Melt the remaining butter in a large frying pan over a moderate heat. Add the onions and cook for 5 minutes, stirring frequently. Stir in the garlic and continue cooking for 1 minute. Remove from the heat and cover the veal rolls with the onion mixture.

6 Return the frying pan to a moderate heat.

Add the wine and 250 ml (8 fl oz) of the beef stock. Cook for 2–3 minutes, stirring constantly. Add the salt and pepper. Remove the wine mixture from the heat and pour over the veal rolls. Cover and transfer the casserole to a preheated oven. Cook for 20–30 minutes.

7 Remove the casserole from the oven. Transfer the veal rolls with a slotted spoon to a working surface. Discard the strings. Arrange the rolls on a heated serving dish. Place the casserole dish over a medium–high heat. Combine the cornflour and remaining stock in a small bowl until smooth. Gradually pour the cornflour mixture in the casserole, stirring constantly. Bring to the boil and simmer until smooth and thick.

8 To serve, coat the veal rolls with the sauce. Garnish with the parsley. Serve with creamed potatoes and a simple stir-fry of green beans and red pepper strips.

[A] The veal rolls may be prepared earlier in the day, covered and chilled.

Top: Vegetable-Braised Veal Roast; bottom; Stuffed Veal Rolls

CASSEROLE OF DUCK WITH RED CABBAGE

SERVES 4
3 tablespoons plain flour
salt
freshly ground black pepper
*1 × 2¼ kg (5 lb) duck, skinned and cut into serving
pieces*
50 g (2 oz) butter
2 tablespoons vegetable oil
1 large onion, peeled and finely chopped
120 ml (4 fl oz) chicken stock
*1 tablespoon chopped fresh basil or ½ teaspoon dried
basil*
*½ head red cabbage, about 750 g (1½ lb), cored and
finely shredded*
1 cooking apple, cored, seeded and chopped
1 garlic clove, peeled and finely chopped
3 tablespoons red wine vinegar
2 tablespoons brown sugar
4 sprigs parsley, to garnish

PREPARATION TIME: 20 minutes
COOKING TIME: 1 hour 45 minutes
OVEN: 180°C, 350°F, Gas Mark 4

1 Combine the flour, salt and pepper on a large plate. Toss the duck pieces thoroughly in the seasoned flour, shaking off the excess, then set aside.

2 Melt 25 g (1 oz) of the butter and the oil in a large frying pan over a medium heat. Place the duck pieces in the pan, then cook for 5–10 minutes, shaking the pan frequently, until browned. Turn the pieces over and continue cooking for another 5–10 minutes, until browned. Remove the pieces from the pan with a slotted spoon and drain on paper towels. Transfer the duck pieces to a large casserole.

3 Add the onion to the frying pan and cook for 10 minutes, stirring frequently, until soft. Transfer the onion to the casserole with a slotted spoon. Blend the chicken stock and basil into the casserole.

4 Melt the remaining butter in the frying pan over a medium heat. Add the red cabbage and cook for 10 minutes, stirring occasionally. Blend in the apple, garlic, vinegar, sugar, salt and pepper into the cabbage. Simmer for 5 minutes, stirring frequently. Add the cabbage to the casserole and cover. Place in a preheated oven and cook for 1 hour, until the duck is tender. [A]

5 Remove the casserole from the oven and taste for salt and pepper. Place the cabbage on a large heated serving platter and top with the duck pieces. Garnish with the parsley sprigs.

[A] The casserole may be cooked earlier in the day, then covered and chilled. Cook at 180°C, 350°F, Gas Mark 4 for 30 minutes, until heated through.

CIVET DE CANARD

SERVES 2
1 × 2 kg (4½ lb) duck, cut into quarters
50 g (2 oz) plain flour
salt
freshly ground black pepper
25 g (1 oz) butter
2 medium onions, peeled and finely chopped
750 ml (1¼ pints) red wine
1 bay leaf
*1 teaspoon fresh thyme leaves or ¼ teaspoon dried
thyme*
12 small onions, peeled
1 tablespoon cornflour
50 ml (2 fl oz) cold duck or chicken stock
1 teaspoon demerara sugar
1 tablespoon chopped fresh parsley, to garnish

PREPARATION TIME: 20 minutes
COOKING TIME: 1¾ hours
OVEN: 180°C, 350°F, Gas Mark 4

1 Prick the duck pieces repeatedly with a fork. Combine the flour, salt and pepper on a plate and coat the duck with the mixture.

2 Melt the butter in a large flameproof casserole over a medium-high heat. Add the duck pieces and cook for 10 minutes on each side until brown. Remove the duck with tongs or a slotted spoon and place on a large plate.

3 Pour off all but 3 tablespoons of the fat in the casserole. Add the onions and cook, stirring frequently, for 5 minutes over a medium heat. Return the duck to the casserole. Blend in the wine, bay leaf and thyme and season with salt and pepper. Transfer the covered casserole to a preheated oven and cook for 1 hour, turning the duck pieces occasionally.

4 Remove the casserole from the oven and stir in the small onions. Cover, return the casserole to the oven and continue cooking for 30 minutes.

5 Remove the casserole from the oven. Skim the fat from the surface. Transfer the duck pieces and onions with tongs or a slotted spoon to a heated platter and keep warm. Place the casserole on a medium heat on the top of the stove. Using a whisk, combine the cornflour and stock in a cup until smooth and pour the mixture into the casserole. Add the sugar. Stirring constantly, cook until the sauce has thickened. Taste and correct seasoning, if necessary.

6 To serve, place the duck pieces on a heated serving dish. Arrange the small onions attractively around the duck. Coat with the sauce, then sprinkle with the parsley.

VEAL, MUSHROOM AND SOURED CREAM CASSEROLE

SERVES 3
40 g (1½ oz) butter
*750 g (1½ lb) boneless veal, cut into 2.5 cm
(1 inch) cubes*
1 medium onion, peeled and finely chopped
1 garlic clove, peeled and finely chopped
225 g (8 oz) field mushrooms, cleaned and sliced
3 tablespoons plain flour
175 ml (6 fl oz) chicken stock
120 ml (4 fl oz) dry white wine
*½ tablespoon fresh thyme leaves or ½ teaspoon dried
thyme*
salt
freshly ground black pepper
175 ml (6 fl oz) soured cream
fresh chives, to garnish

PREPARATION TIME: 25 minutes
COOKING TIME: 2 hours
OVEN: 150°C, 300°F, Gas Mark 2

1 Melt the butter in a large frying pan over a medium heat. When hot, add the veal cubes. Stirring frequently, cook for 5–10 minutes, until browned on all sides. Remove the cubes with a slotted spoon and place in a casserole.

2 Add the onion, garlic and mushrooms to the pan. Cook, stirring frequently, for 10 minutes.

3 Sprinkle the flour on the onion mixture. Cook, stirring constantly, for 2–3 minutes. Gradually blend in the stock, wine, thyme, salt and pepper. Cook, stirring frequently, for 2–3 minutes. Remove the pan from the heat and let cool for 2 minutes. Blend the soured cream into the sauce. Pour the sauce over the meat, stir well, then cover. [A] Transfer the casserole to a preheated oven and cook for 1½ hours.

4 To serve, garnish with the chives. Buttered flat noodles are a good accompaniment.

[A] The casserole can be prepared several hours ahead of time, covered and kept chilled. Simmer gently for 10 minutes before proceeding with the recipe.

From the top: Casserole of Duck; Civet de Canard; Veal, Mushroom and Soured Cream Casserole

STUFFED CHICKEN ROLLS WITH TARRAGON SAUCE

SERVES 6

FOR THE TARRAGON SAUCE:
15 g (½ oz) butter
2 shallots, peeled and finely chopped
250 ml (8 fl oz) white wine
475 ml (16 fl oz) chicken stock
475 ml (16 fl oz) double cream
2 tablespoons finely chopped fresh tarragon or
2 teaspoons dried tarragon
salt
freshly ground white pepper

FOR THE CHICKEN:
15 g (½ oz) butter
2 medium carrots, peeled and cut into fine julienne strips
1 medium leek, peeled and cut into fine julienne strips
6 large chicken breasts, halved, skinned, boned and flattened to an even thickness
1 litre (1¾ pints) hot chicken stock

PREPARATION TIME: 35 minutes
COOKING TIME: 1 hour
OVEN: 180°C, 350°F, Gas Mark 4

From the left: Stuffed Chicken Rolls with Tarragon Sauce; Turkey and Chestnut Casserole

1 For the sauce, melt the butter in a large saucepan over a moderate heat. Add the shallots and cook for 3 minutes until soft but not browned. Add the wine, then increase the heat to high. Boil the mixture until it has reduced to 2 tablespoons. Stir in the chicken stock, then boil until the mixture has reduced to 120 ml (4 fl oz). Add the cream and tarragon, then continue boiling until the sauce has thickened to a coating consistency. Season with salt and pepper, then set aside. [A]

2 For the chicken, melt the butter in a frying pan over a medium heat. Add the carrots and leek, then cook for 1 minute, stirring constantly. Remove from the heat and set aside.

3 Place 1 flattened chicken breast half, skinned side down, on a working surface. Season with the salt and pepper. Arrange one sixth of the carrot and leek mixture near one edge of the chicken. Roll the chicken up tightly to enclose the vegetables, then tie with string to secure. Repeat with the remaining chicken breasts and vegetables. [A]

4 Transfer the chicken rolls to a large casserole. Add the stock. Cover the casserole and place in a preheated oven. Cook for 25 minutes until the rolls are firm to the touch.

5 While the rolls are cooking, reheat the sauce over a gentle heat. Stir frequently.

6 Remove the casserole from the oven and transfer the rolls to a working surface. Cut the string off the rolls. Cut each roll diagonally into 4 pieces. Pour the sauce on to 6 plates, just coating the bottom. Arrange 1 cut roll, vegetable filling facing upwards, on the sauce. Repeat with the five remaining rolls. Serve immediately with sautéed potatoes and steamed spinach.

[A] The sauce and chicken rolls can be prepared earlier in the day, covered and chilled.

TURKEY AND CHESTNUT CASSEROLE

FOR THE MARINADE:
600 ml (1 pint) dry white wine
50 ml (2 fl oz) white wine vinegar
1 medium onion, peeled and sliced
1 garlic clove, peeled and finely chopped
2 tablespoons fresh thyme leaves or 1 teaspoon dried thyme
1 bay leaf
1 lemon slice
salt
12 black peppercorns, crushed
1¼ kg (2½ lb) boneless raw turkey meat, skinned and cut into 2.5 cm (1 inch) cubes

TO FINISH THE CASSEROLE:
2 tablespoons vegetable oil
50 g (2 oz) butter
1 medium onion, peeled and sliced
1 garlic clove, peeled and finely chopped
100 g (4 oz) button mushrooms, cleaned and left whole
40 g (1½ oz) plain flour
150 ml (¼ pint) turkey or chicken stock
2 tablespoons cranberry jelly
freshly ground black pepper
225 g (8 oz) cooked peeled chestnuts
fresh parsley sprigs, to garnish

PREPARATION TIME: 40 minutes, plus marinating
COOKING TIME: 2 hours
OVEN: 180°C, 350°F, Gas Mark 4

1 Combine all the ingredients for the marinade, except the turkey pieces, in a large, shallow casserole. Add the turkey, tossing well to coat. Cover and chill overnight.

2 To finish the casserole, lift out the turkey pieces from the marinade. Pat dry with paper towels and set aside. Strain the marinade and reserve.

3 Heat the oil in a large frying pan over a medium heat. Add the turkey pieces and brown on all sides, turning frequently. Remove from the casserole with a slotted spoon and place in a large flameproof casserole.

4 Add the butter to the frying pan. Melt over a moderate heat, then add the onion and garlic. Cook, stirring frequently, for 5 minutes. Add the mushrooms, then continue cooking, stirring occasionally, for another 5 minutes.

5 Blend the flour into the frying pan. Cook, stirring constantly, for 2–3 minutes. Using a whisk, gradually blend in the reserved marinade and stock. Bring to the boil, stirring constantly. Remove from the heat, then add the cranberry jelly, salt and pepper. Pour the sauce over the turkey pieces and cover. [A] Cook the casserole in a preheated oven for 1 hour.

6 Remove the casserole from the oven and transfer the turkey pieces, mushrooms and onions with a slotted spoon to a heated serving dish. Set aside and keep warm.

7 Place the casserole over a medium-high heat on the stove. Bring to the boil and reduce by a third. Add the chestnuts, lower the heat to medium, then simmer for 5 minutes.

8 To serve, coat the turkey mixture with the chestnut sauce and garnish with the parsley.

[A] The casserole can be made earlier in the day, covered and chilled. Simmer for 10 minutes before proceeding with the recipe.

CHICKEN FRICASSÉE

SERVES 6

350 g (12 oz) frozen puff pastry, thawed
1 egg, beaten
1 teaspoon milk
1¾ kg (4 lb) whole chicken, trussed, giblets removed
1.75 litres (3 pints) chicken stock
1.75 litres (3 pints) water
1 medium onion, peeled and studded with 4 cloves
1 celery stalk, chopped
2 sprigs parsley
salt
6 whole black peppercorns
75 g (3 oz) butter
8 tablespoons plain flour
50 ml (2 fl oz) dry white wine
50 ml (2 fl oz) double cream
1 tablespoon finely chopped fresh tarragon
1 teaspoon Worcestershire sauce
freshly ground white pepper
2 large carrots, peeled, diced and cooked crisp-tender
75 g (3 oz) frozen peas, thawed or fresh, cooked
crisp-tender

PREPARATION TIME: 40 minutes
COOKING TIME: 2¼ hours
OVEN: 220°C, 425°F, Gas Mark 7; then:
180°C, 350°F, Gas Mark 4

1 Roll out the pastry to a thickness of 5 mm (¼ inch). Cut out 12 teardrop shapes, each about 5 cm (2 inches) long. Let rest 10 minutes.

2 Combine the egg and milk, then lightly brush the tops of the pastry only with the egg mixture. Place on a baking sheet and cook in a preheated oven for 10 minutes. Reduce the heat and cook for 15–20 minutes, until golden brown. If the pastry colours too fast, cover with a sheet of greaseproof paper. Remove the pastry from the oven and let cool.

3 Bring the chicken, stock, water, studded onion, celery, parsley, salt and peppercorns to the boil in a large saucepan. Reduce the heat and simmer, partially covered, for 60 minutes. Skim off the scum when necessary.

4 Remove the saucepan from the heat. Discard the onion, celery and parsley. Let the chicken cool in the stock. [A]

5 Remove the skin and bones from the chicken and discard. Cut the chicken into bite-sized pieces. Strain the stock and skim off the fat. Measure 650 ml (22 fl oz) of the stock and reserve. Save the rest for another use.

6 Melt the butter in a large saucepan over a moderate heat. Blend in the flour and, stirring continuously, cook for 2–3 minutes. Gradually add the reserved stock and white wine. Cook for 5–10 minutes, stirring continuously, until smooth and thick. Add the cream, Worcestershire sauce, thyme, salt and pepper, then heat through. Remove the mixture from the heat. Blend in the chicken, carrots and peas. Transfer the fricassée to a casserole and cover. Cook in a preheated oven for 30–35 minutes.

7 To serve, garnish the fricassée with the pastry cut-outs.

[A] The chicken can be cooked up to 1 day in advance, covered and kept chilled. The fricassée can be prepared earlier in the day, covered and kept chilled. Allow the fricassée to stand at room temperature for 1 hour before continuing.

POULET GRANDMÈRE

SERVES 6

3 tablespoons olive oil
100 g (4 oz) unsmoked bacon, rinded, cut into strips
2 medium onions, peeled and thinly sliced
2 medium carrots, peeled and cut into 5 cm (2 inch)
barrel-shaped pieces
2 × 1 kg (2¼ lb) chickens, jointed into 6 pieces
salt
freshly ground black pepper
25 g (1 oz) butter
2 tablespoons plain flour
4 tablespoons brandy
150 ml (¼ pint) dry white wine
900 ml (1½ pints) chicken stock
1 tablespoon fresh thyme or 1 teaspoon dried thyme
2 teaspoons finely chopped fresh parsley
1 bay leaf, crumbled
4 large potatoes, peeled and cubed
1.2 litres (2 pints) cold water
50 g (2 oz) butter
225 g (8 oz) small button mushrooms, cleaned, stems
trimmed
1 tablespoon olive oil
2 tablespoons cornflour
4 tablespoons chicken stock

PREPARATION TIME: 45 minutes
COOKING TIME: 2½ hours
OVEN: 180°C, 350°F, Gas Mark 4

1 Heat one tablespoon of the oil in a large frying pan. Add the bacon and cook for 5–10 minutes. Remove to drain on a paper towel. [A]

2 Cook the onions and carrots in the pan for 20 minutes. Remove from the pan with a slotted spoon and set aside. [A]

Opposite, from the top:
Chicken Fricassée;
Poulet Grandmère

148

3 Season the chicken pieces with the salt and pepper. Heat the remaining oil and the butter in the frying pan. Add the chicken pieces and cook for 10 minutes until lightly browned. Sprinkle over the flour and cook for 5–10 minutes, turning occasionally until the flour has browned. Return the onions and carrots to the pan.

4 Warm the brandy in a flameproof ladle and pour over the chicken pieces. Carefully set alight. If the flames become too vigorous, cover the pan with a tight lid. When the flames have died, remove the chicken to a large flameproof casserole.

5 Increase the heat to high. Add the wine to the frying pan and bring to the boil. Blend in the chicken stock, thyme, parsley and bay leaf and bring to a simmer. Pour the sauce over the chicken pieces. Cover and cook in a preheated oven for 45 minutes. [A]

6 Bring the potato cubes and water to the boil in a saucepan. Drain the potatoes in a colander. [A]

7 Melt 25 g (1 oz) of the butter in a medium frying pan. Add the mushrooms then cook for 5 minutes, stirring constantly. Remove the mushrooms and set aside. [A]

8 When the chicken is cooked, remove the casserole from the oven. Transfer the chicken pieces to a clean flameproof casserole. Strain the vegetables and sauce through a sieve into a medium frying pan. Add the vegetables to the chicken pieces and keep warm.

9 Bring the sauce to the boil over a high heat. Reduce the heat and place the pan half off the heat so that only one side continues to boil. Remove the fat and impurities which form on the still side with a spoon. Repeat until the sauce is free from fat. Mix the cornflour and chicken stock smoothly in a cup and stir into the sauce. Bring the sauce to the boil and cook for 2–3 minutes.

10 Blend the sauce into the casserole. Stir in the mushrooms. Place the casserole over a moderate heat and bring to a simmer. Cook for 20 minutes, until heated through.

11 Heat the remaining butter and oil in a large frying pan, add the potatoes and toss until brown. Lower the heat and add the bacon. Cook for 1 minute, then scatter over the casserole.

[A] The bacon, onions, carrots, chicken and garnishes can be prepared earlier in the day, covered and kept chilled until needed.

QUAIL CASSEROLE

1.25 litres (2¼ pints) water
225 g (8 oz) bacon, rinded and cut into strips
75 g (3 oz) butter
8 quail, about 100 g (4 oz) each
475 ml (16 fl oz) chicken stock
250 ml (8 fl oz) Madeira wine
salt
freshly ground black pepper
275 g (10 oz) button mushrooms, cleaned and quartered
15 g (½ oz) porcini mushrooms, reconstituted for 30 minutes in 250 ml (8 fl oz) warm water, then drained well and chopped
3 tablespoons cornflour
120 ml (4 fl oz) double or whipping cream

PREPARATION TIME: 20 minutes, plus 30 minutes reconstitution
COOKING TIME: 1¾ hours

Though game is traditionally eaten 'high' or hung for a period of time, quail must be eaten fresh. High quail can have a powerful smell that is not very appetizing.

1 Bring the water to the boil in a medium saucepan. Add the bacon and cook for 1–2 minutes. Remove the pan from the heat, drain the bacon in a colander and set aside.

2 Melt 50 g (2 oz) of the butter in a flameproof casserole over a medium-low heat. Add the bacon and, stirring occasionally, cook for 10 minutes. Add the quail to the casserole and brown on all sides, turning the quail frequently. Drain off the excess fat and discard. Blend in the stock, 120 ml (4 fl oz) of the Madeira, salt and pepper. Cover the casserole. Cook over a medium-low heat for 30 minutes.

3 While the quail are cooking, melt the remaining butter in a large frying pan over a medium heat. Add the button and reconstituted porcini mushrooms. Cover and cook for 10 minutes, shaking the pan frequently. Remove from the heat and set aside.

4 When the quail have cooked for 30 minutes, add the mushrooms to the casserole. Cover and continue cooking for another 20 minutes. [A]

5 Transfer the quail to a heated serving platter and keep warm. Increase the heat under the casserole to high. Combine the cornflour and remaining Madeira in a cup until smooth. Using a whisk, stir into the casserole. Add the cream and let the mixture come to the boil. Boil for 2–3 minutes. Taste and adjust the seasoning, if necessary, then remove the sauce from the heat.

6 To serve, pour the sauce over the quail.

[A] The casserole can be made several hours in advance, covered and kept chilled. Simmer for 15 minutes before proceeding with the recipe.

PHEASANT AND PORT CASSEROLE

SERVES 6

FOR THE MARINADE:
450 ml (¾ pint) port wine
1 large onion, peeled and sliced
1 large carrot, peeled and thinly sliced
2 sticks celery, chopped
1 garlic clove, peeled and finely chopped
1 tablespoon fresh thyme leaves or ½ teaspoon dried thyme
4 juniper berries, crushed
1 bay leaf, crumbled
salt
freshly ground black pepper
2 pheasants, about 1¼ kg (2½ lb) each, skinned and jointed

TO FINISH:
75 g (3 oz) butter
15 g (½ oz) dried porcini mushrooms, reconstituted in 250 ml (8 fl oz) warm water for 30 minutes, then drained well and chopped
225 g (8 oz) field mushrooms, cleaned and sliced
25 g (1 oz) plain flour
300 ml (½ pint) pheasant or chicken stock
150 ml (¼ pint) double cream
1 tablespoon finely chopped fresh parsley, to garnish

PREPARATION TIME: 25 minutes, plus marinating
COOKING TIME: 1½ hours
OVEN: 180°C, 350°F, Gas Mark 4

Porcini mushrooms (meaning 'little pig'), used in this recipe, are dried Italian mushrooms. If they are unavailable, substitute an additional 225 g (8 oz) of field mushrooms.

1 Combine the port, onion, carrot, celery, garlic, thyme, juniper berries, bay leaf, salt and pepper in a deep bowl. Add the pheasant pieces and coat them evenly with the marinade. Cover and chill overnight. [A]

2 Remove the pheasant pieces from the marinade and pat dry with paper towels. Strain and reserve the marinade.

3 Heat 50 g (2 oz) of the butter in a large frying pan over a medium-high heat. Brown the pheasant pieces in the butter, turning occasionally, for 10 minutes. Transfer the pieces with a slotted spoon or tongs to a flameproof casserole. Set aside.

4 Melt the remaining butter in the frying pan over a medium heat. Add the porcini and field mushrooms. Cook, stirring occasionally, for 5 minutes. Blend in the flour and, stirring continuously, cook for 2–3 minutes. Lower the heat. Using a whisk, gradually add the stock and reserved marinade. Cook, whisking continuously, until the sauce comes to the boil and has slightly thickened. Remove the sauce from the heat and pour over the pheasant. Cover and cook in a preheated oven for 1 hour. [A]

5 Remove the casserole from the oven. Trans-fer the pheasant pieces with a slotted spoon or tongs to a heated serving dish. Keep warm in the oven while making the sauce.

6 To finish, pour the sauce into a medium saucepan. Bring to the boil over a high heat. Add the cream and simmer for 2–3 minutes. Remove the sauce from the heat and pour over the pheasant pieces.

7 To serve, garnish the pheasant with the parsley. Crisp potato pancakes and steamed broccoli would go well with this dish.

[A] The pheasants may be marinated for up to 3 days, turning the pieces over daily. The casserole may be cooked earlier in the day, then covered and chilled. Reheat in a 180°C, 350°F, Gas Mark 4 oven for 30 minutes or until heated through, before proceeding with the recipe.

From the left: Quail Casserole; Pheasant and Port Casserole

BRITTANY FISH CASSEROLE

SERVES 8

FOR THE FISH BASE:
1¾ kg (4 lb) fish bones, rinsed and broken into small pieces
4.75 litres (9 pints) water
450 ml (¾ pint) fish stock
300 ml (½ pint) dry white wine
4 medium onions, peeled and sliced
1 carrot, peeled and sliced
12 parsley sprigs
1 bay leaf
1 tablespoon chopped fresh thyme leaves or
½ teaspoon dried thyme

FOR THE FISH AND VEGETABLES:
4 tablespoons lemon juice
2 tablespoons finely chopped fresh chives
1 tablespoon finely chopped fresh parsley
1 tablespoon finely chopped fresh tarragon
500 g (1¼ lb) skinned and boned salmon steaks, cut into 2.5 cm (1 inch) cubes
450 g (1 lb) skinned and boned halibut steaks, cut into 2.5 cm (1 inch) cubes
450 g (1 lb) thick sole fillets, cut into 1 cm (1½ inch) strips
450 g (1 lb) freshly shelled small scallops
225 g (8 oz) large raw prawns, peeled and deveined
450 g (1 lb) mussels, scrubbed and debearded
2 medium shallots, peeled and finely chopped
250 ml (8 fl oz) water
100 g (4 oz) cauliflower florets
100 g (4 oz) broccoli florets

TO FINISH:
8 tablespoons cornflour
350 ml (12 fl oz) double or whipping cream
salt
freshly ground white pepper
1 tablespoon finely chopped fresh parsley

PREPARATION TIME: 40 minutes
COOKING TIME: 90 minutes

This fish stew is unusual, and appreciated both in warmer and cooler months. Best of all, if everything is prepared in advance, it is ready within 15 minutes. Bringing this casserole to the table with the appearance of little effort will definitely be a hit with your guests.

1 To make the fish base, place the fish bones, water, stock, 250 ml (8 fl oz) of the wine, onions, carrot, parsley, bay leaf and thyme in a large saucepan. Bring to the boil over a high heat, then reduce the heat and simmer for 45 minutes. Crush the bones occasionally with a wooden spoon while simmering. Ladle the mixture through a strainer lined with several layers of dampened muslin cloth into a large, heavy saucepan. Cover and set aside. [A]

2 For the fish, blend together the lemon juice, chives, parsley and tarragon in a small bowl. Combine the salmon, halibut, sole, scallops and prawns in a large, shallow pan. Pour the lemon juice mixture over the fish and toss to coat. Cover and chill. [A]

3 Combine the mussels, remaining white wine and shallots in a medium saucepan. Cover and cook over a medium-high heat for 3–4 minutes. Using a slotted spoon, remove any opened mussels to a large bowl. Cover and continue cooking the remaining mussels for 2 minutes. Remove the remaining opened mussels to the bowl. Discard any mussels that do not open. Reserve the cooking liquid. Remove the mussels from the shell, discarding the shells. Cover and set aside. Ladle the cooking liquid into the fish base through a strainer lined with several layers of dampened muslin cloth. Cover and set aside. [A]

4 Bring the water to the boil in a medium saucepan. Add the cauliflower florets and cook for 3–4 minutes, until crisp-tender. Remove with a slotted spoon and place in a colander under cold running water. When the cauliflower is cool, drain well, then cover and set aside. Add the broccoli florets to the boiling water and cook for 2–3 minutes, until crisp-tender. Remove with a slotted spoon and place in a colander under cold running water. When the broccoli is cool, drain well, then cover and set aside. Ladle the vegetable liquid into the fish base through a strainer lined with several layers of dampened muslin cloth. Cover and set aside. [A]

5 To finish the casserole, drain the marinated fish and shellfish. Place in a large flameproof casserole. Bring the fish base to a boil over high heat. Place the cornflour in a medium bowl then, using a whisk, gradually blend in the cream until smooth. Whisk the cornflour mixture into the fish base and, stirring continuously, cook for 5 minutes until smooth and thick. Pour the fish base into the casserole. Place the casserole over a medium-high heat and cook for 5 minutes. Add the mussels, cauliflower and broccoli, then heat through. Add the salt and pepper to taste, then serve immediately.

[A] The fish base, marinated fish and shellfish, mussels and blanched vegetables can be prepared earlier in the day, covered and kept chilled until required.

PRAWN GUMBO WITH RICE

SERVES 8
2 tablespoons oil
2 sticks celery, finely sliced
1 onion, peeled and diced
1 green pepper, seeded and diced
1 garlic clove, peeled and crushed
1 tablespoon Worcestershire sauce
1 × 400 g (14 oz) can tomatoes
300 ml (½ pint) tomato juice
salt
freshly ground black pepper
100 g (4 oz) long-grain rice
100 g (4 oz) okra, stems removed, sliced
225 g (8 oz) peeled prawns, fresh or frozen
225 g (8 oz) dressed crabmeat, fresh or frozen
4 tablespoons dry sherry

TO GARNISH:
garlic croûtons
chopped fresh parsley

PREPARATION TIME: 30 minutes
COOKING TIME: 1¼ hours
OVEN: 160°C, 325°F, Gas Mark 3

1 Heat the oil in a flameproof casserole and cook the celery, onion and pepper gently for 5 minutes.

2 Add the garlic, Worcestershire sauce, tomatoes and tomato juice, and season with salt and pepper.

3 Stir in the rice and okra, and bring gently to simmering point. Cover, and cook in a preheated oven for 1 hour.

4 Gently stir in the prawns, crabmeat and sherry (if the rice looks a little dry, add a little more tomato juice).

5 Re-cover, and return to the oven for 15 minutes. Pour into a heated serving dish, group the croûtons at either end and sprinkle with the chopped fresh parsley.

Top: Brittany Fish Casserole; bottom: Prawn Gumbo with Rice

NEW ENGLAND OYSTERS

450 g (1 lb) freshly shelled oysters, with 120 ml
(4 fl oz) of the oyster liquor reserved
40 g (1½ oz) melted butter
100 g (4 oz) salted cracker crumbs
freshly ground black pepper
Tabasco sauce
120 ml (4 fl oz) double or whipping cream

PREPARATION TIME: 20 minutes
COOKING TIME: 30 minutes
OVEN: 200°C, 400°F, Gas Mark 6

This recipe breaks 2 rules about oysters. Purists will object to cooking oysters. They maintain that an oyster is best when eaten raw – and heaven forbid that you should add salt, cocktail sauce or vinegar to these freshly shelled morsels!

The second broken rule is the peculiarity of adding cracker crumbs to this recipe. In fact, scalloped oysters were a virtual institution in England and North America in the 1800s when a glut of oysters tested cooks' ingenuity – thus the evolution of this dish. Today, it is expensive, but the oysters retain their fresh smell of the sea and the crumbs add a special richness.

1 Place a sieve lined with a double thickness of muslin cloth over a medium bowl. Drain the oyster liquor in the sieve and reserve. Remove any pieces of shell or grit from the oysters. Rinse briefly, then drain well in the sieve.

2 Combine the reserved oyster liquor with the cream. Set aside.

3 Grease a medium casserole with 1 tablespoon of the melted butter. Place a third of the crumbs on the bottom of the dish. Arrange half of the drained oysters over the crumbs. Season with the pepper and Tabasco sauce. Pour half of the oyster liquor mixture over the oysters. Top evenly with another third of the crumbs. Arrange the remaining oysters evenly over the crumbs. Season with the pepper and Tabasco sauce. Pour the remaining oyster liquor over the oysters. Top with the remaining crumbs and dot with the remaining butter. [A]

4 Place the casserole uncovered in a preheated oven. Cook for 30 minutes, until the cream is bubbly and the crumbs are golden brown.

[A] Can be prepared up to 2 hours in advance, covered and chilled. Allow the casserole to return to room temperature before cooking.

Clockwise from top:
New England Oysters;
Avocado Seafood
Casserole; Scallop
Casserole

AVOCADO SEAFOOD CASSEROLE

SERVES 8
120 g (4½ oz) butter
1 large ripe avocado pear, halved, stoned, peeled and cubed
2 teaspoons lemon juice
350 g (12 oz) cooked white crabmeat
350 g (12 oz) cooked peeled prawns
350 g (12 oz) cooked scallops, halved if large
175 g (6 oz) onion, peeled and finely chopped
100 g (4 oz) plain flour
400 ml (14 fl oz) single cream
400 ml (14 fl oz) milk
1 teaspoon Dijon mustard
175 g (6 oz) Gruyère cheese, grated
1 tablespoon fresh thyme leaves or ½ teaspoon dried thyme
salt
freshly ground white pepper

TO GARNISH:
½ avocado pear, halved, stoned, peeled and cut into a fan shape
1 sprig parsley (optional)

PREPARATION TIME: 15 minutes
COOKING TIME: 50–55 minutes
OVEN: 180°C, 350°F, Gas Mark 4

1 Grease a 23 cm × 33 cm (9 inch × 13 inch) casserole dish with 15 g (½ oz) of the butter. Set aside. Toss the avocado with the lemon juice in a medium bowl. Combine the avocado mixture, crabmeat, prawns and scallops in the casserole. Set aside.

2 Melt the remaining butter in a large saucepan over a moderate heat. Cook the onion, stirring frequently, for 10 minutes or until soft and golden. Lower the heat, then blend in the flour. Stirring constantly, cook for 2–3 minutes. Using a whisk, gradually add the cream, milk and mustard. Increase the heat to medium and cook for 5 minutes, stirring constantly, until smooth and thick. Stir the cheese into the sauce. Remove the saucepan from the heat, then add the thyme, salt and pepper. Gently blend the sauce into the seafood mixture. [A]

3 Bake the casserole in a preheated oven for 30–40 minutes, until heated through.

4 Garnish with the avocado fan and parsley, if liked. Serve with rice and a tomato salad.

[A] Can be made several hours in advance, covered and kept chilled.

SCALLOP CASSEROLE

SERVES 6
FOR THE COURT BOUILLON:
8 small onions, peeled
4 carrots, peeled and sliced
3 celery stalks, sliced
1 leek, white part only, chopped
12 parsley sprigs
1 bay leaf
1 sprig fresh thyme or ¼ teaspoon dried thyme
1 sprig fresh tarragon or ¼ teaspoon dried tarragon
⅛ teaspoon ground coriander
⅛ teaspoon saffron threads
1 clove
1 pinch cayenne pepper
salt
freshly ground white pepper
2.25 litres (4 pints) water

FOR THE SCALLOPS:
1½ kg (3 lb) freshly shelled scallops with coral
⅛ teaspoon saffron threads
250 ml (8 fl oz) white vermouth
250 ml (8 fl oz) double or whipping cream
¼ teaspoon lemon juice
1 tablespoon finely chopped fresh chervil
1 tablespoon finely chopped fresh chives

PREPARATION TIME: 30 minutes, plus cooling
COOKING TIME: 45–50 minutes

1 Place all the ingredients for the court bouillon in a large saucepan. Cover and bring to the boil over a high heat. Boil for 10 minutes. Remove from the heat and let stand until cool. [A]

2 Place the scallops in one layer in a large flameproof casserole. Heat the court bouillon until just boiling. Strain over the scallops. Cook over a low-medium heat for 4 minutes.

3 Remove the casserole from the heat. Strain the court bouillon into a large saucepan and reserve. Cover the scallops and keep warm.

4 Boil the court bouillon over a high heat until it has reduced to 250 ml (8 fl oz). Remove 25 ml (1 fl oz) and soak the saffron threads in this.

5 Add the vermouth and cream to the court bouillon. Return the sauce to the boil. Add the lemon juice and the saffron mixture. Stir in the chervil and chives. Pour the sauce over the scallops, then cover and let stand for 5 minutes.

[A] The court bouillon can be made several hours in advance, covered and kept chilled.

SEAFOOD AND WILD RICE CASSEROLE

SERVES 6

FOR THE RICE:
275 g (10 oz) raw, wild rice
750 ml (1¼ pints) beef stock
50 g (2 oz) butter
salt
freshly ground black pepper

MUSHROOM SAUCE:
35 g (1¼ oz) butter
100 g (4 oz) button mushrooms, cleaned and sliced
4 tablespoons finely chopped shallots
1½ teaspoons curry powder
1½ tablespoons fresh thyme leaves or ¾ teaspoon dried thyme
1½ tablespoons plain flour
120 ml (4 fl oz) single cream
120 ml (4 fl oz) milk
175 ml (6 fl oz) double or whipping cream
2 tablespoons Chinese oyster sauce

FOR THE SEAFOOD:
225 g (8 oz) cooked, shelled prawns
225 g (8 oz) cooked white crabmeat
sprig fresh thyme, to garnish

PREPARATION TIME: 30 minutes
COOKING TIME: 40 minutes, plus 1 hour for the rice
OVEN: 160°C, 325°F, Gas Mark 3

Wild rice is not rice, but the long, narrow, dark brown grain of a native American grass, *Zizania aquatica*. Because of the difficulty in harvesting the rice – it has not been domesticated and it grows in water – it can be prohibitively expensive, even in its native country. If wild rice is unavailable, brown rice may be used instead. Follow the packet's instructions for cooking the rice, then proceed with the recipe from the mushroom sauce.

1 For the rice, place the rice, stock, butter, salt and pepper in the top of a double boiler. Insert the top over boiling water, cover and steam the rice for 45 minutes to 1 hour over a medium-low heat. If necessary, add more boiling water to the bottom of the double boiler while cooking. Remove the double boiler from the heat and fluff up the rice with a fork. Gently stir in the butter. Set aside. [A]

2 For the mushroom sauce, melt the butter over a medium heat in a small saucepan. Add the mushrooms, shallots, salt and pepper and cook for 10 minutes, stirring frequently. Stir in the curry powder and thyme. Blend in the flour and cook for 2–3 minutes, stirring constantly. Using a whisk, gradually stir in the cream and milk. Cook until thick and smooth. Blend in the double cream, oyster sauce, salt and pepper. Cook, stirring, for 5 minutes. Set aside. [A]

3 Spoon half of the wild rice mixture on to the bottom of an oval casserole. Cover evenly with the prawns and crab. Add the remaining rice mixture, smoothing the top down. Spoon the mushroom sauce over the rice. Transfer the casserole to a preheated oven and cook for 30 minutes, until heated through.

5 Before serving, garnish the casserole with sprigs of fresh thyme.

[A] The wild rice can be prepared earlier in the day, covered and kept chilled.

CRAB-STUFFED SOLE ROLLS

SERVES 6
6 × 100 g (4 oz) skinned fillets of sole
250 ml (8 fl oz) dry white wine

FOR THE STUFFING:
40 g (1½ oz) butter
1 medium onion, peeled and finely chopped
100 g (4 oz) mushrooms, cleaned and chopped
2 garlic cloves, peeled and finely chopped (optional)
225 g (8 oz) cooked white crabmeat
25 g (1 oz) chopped parsley
2 tablespoons dried breadcrumbs
dash cayenne pepper
salt
freshly ground white pepper

FOR THE SAUCE:
50 g (2 oz) butter
4 tablespoons plain flour
250 ml (8 fl oz) fish stock
250 ml (8 fl oz) single cream
225 g (8 oz) Gruyère cheese, grated
2 tablespoons lemon juice
½ teaspoon paprika

TO GARNISH:
1 tablespoon finely chopped fresh parsley
1 tablespoon sieved hard-boiled egg yolk

PREPARATION TIME: 20 minutes, plus marinating
COOKING TIME: 40 minutes
OVEN: 180°C, 350°F, Gas Mark 4

1 Place the sole fillets in a shallow pan, then cover with the white wine. Marinate for 1

hour, then remove the fillets. Reserve the wine.

2 For the stuffing, melt the butter in a large frying pan over a moderate heat. Add the onion, mushrooms and garlic, if using, then cook for 10 minutes, stirring occasionally. Remove the onion mixture from the heat and transfer to a large bowl. Stir in the crabmeat, parsley, breadcrumbs, cayenne, salt and pepper.

3 To stuff the fillets, place ⅙ of the stuffing on each fillet. Roll up the fillet to enclose the stuffing. [A]

4 Carefully transfer the fillets, seam side down, to a large casserole dish. Cover the fillets with the reserved wine. Cut a sheet of greaseproof paper to cover the casserole dish, put it on the casserole, then transfer the fish to a preheated oven. Cook for 10 minutes.

5 While the fish is cooking, make the sauce. Melt the butter in a medium saucepan over a medium heat. Blend in the flour then, stirring constantly, cook for 2–3 minutes. Using a whisk, gradually add the stock and cream and cook until smooth and thick, stirring constantly. Blend in the cheese and cook until just melted. Remove the sauce from the heat, then add the lemon juice, salt and pepper.

6 Remove the fillets from the oven. Stir the liquid from the fish into the sauce. Pour the sauce evenly over the fillets. Sprinkle with the paprika. Return the fillets to the oven and continue cooking for another 15 minutes.

7 Remove the casserole from the oven and serve the rolls garnished with the parsley and egg yolk. Rice and a green salad would go well with this casserole.

[A] The fillets can be stuffed in advance, covered and kept chilled.

From the left: Seafood and Wild Rice Casserole; Crab-Stuffed Sole Rolls

INDEX

Acknowledgments

Photography: Vernon Morgan
Photographic stylist: Sarah Wiley
Text illustration: Julia Rowntree
Cover illustration: Christine Robins, Garden Studio
Food prepared for photography by Nicola Diggins and Kate Benson

The publishers would also like to thank David Mellor, 4 Sloane Square, London SW1 (tel. 01-730 4259), 26 James Street, Covent Garden, London WC2 (tel. 01-379 6947) and 66 King Street, Manchester M2 (tel. 061-834 7023), for lending equipment used in the photography in this book.